MW00380991

WordPress for Beginners 2016

A Visual Step-by-Step Guide to Mastering Wordpress

Updated September 2016

Dr. Andy Williams

http://ezseonews.com

What people are saying about this book:

"I work in the education department at one of the top academic institutions in the U.S. and if I could hire Dr. Williams to write all of my online training, I wouldn't hesitate..." **Laurie**

"Wow! From someone who is not a beginner to Wordpress." **Albert J**

"Definitely the go-to guide! Since Wordpress is a pretty easy format to get started on, I was able to make some progress. Then I found Wordpress for Beginners and WOW - my progress took off. Having a visual guide with extensive photos really helps those of us who are visual learners. But the best thing to me is that Williams not only describes what to do and how to do it, he explains why you should do it. I'm not a professional tech person and this book is exactly what I needed. I suspect I will continue to refer to it in the future. Highly recommended." **Amazon Customer**

"Nailed It. I have been trying to install a working blog from time to time for the last four years, and of course have read various books on the subject. It always got more complicated, with dashboards, PHP, SQL, SEO, or a shared Wordpress site. This is the one book that does it flawlessly, and the installation actually works just as shown. The screen shots are accurate and most helpful as you step through each learning segment. Having written several technical how-to manuals myself, I recognize a remarkably well structured and logical sequence of easy to learn, bite sized topics." **Terry O'Hara**

"If you want to have a website but don't know how, this book by Dr. Andy Williams will take you by the hand and walk you through the process of setting up your own blog correctly. He tells you not only exactly how to do it, but also explains the why you are taking the steps he walks you through. The instructions and visuals are clear and easy for anyone to follow." **J. Tanner**

"I Would Give This Book a 5 Plus. I literally started at page one and built my website from scratch without any prior experience because *of this book. It was very easy to read and was laid out in a very logical, step by step order. I would recommend it without hesitation. I was so impressed with this book that I went and ordered several other of the authors books relating to developing an online presence."* **GP**

"Clear, practical, and very helpful, Wordpress for Beginners takes the reader step by step through the essentials of organizing your online world. Dr. Williams is a great writer and an excellent teacher. Highly recommended!" **Dr. James A. Holmund**

"Great Lessons From a Great Teacher. Andy Williams really has a knack for organizing information in a clear, concise, and to-the-point manner. It is only a matter of following his excellent advice, and you will have a functioning Wordpress site up and running in no time." **Prufrock**

"Why can't all guides be like this?" **B J Burton**

"Exemplary teaching. This book is a model of good teaching. Clear, uncluttered, direct. It takes you through the process with admirable clarity. I bought a printed guide to Word Press for twice the price which left me utterly confused - this book should be used as an example of how to teach. Very highly recommended." **Amazon Customer**

"An excellent book. I logged into my account and just followed the book page by page and in no time all I had a Website mapped out and running. The book is easy to follow and you very quickly learn how Wordpress works and how it can be used for writing Blogs, conventional Websites and even combined ones if you are so inclined. This really is an excellent book to have in your programming library and is of great value in helping to steer through the morass of misinformation about Wordpress on the web. I have just ordered the paperback version to have by my side which I anticipate will become well-worn into the future." **Dr. A F Gerrard**

"Quite simply the best advice I've found............ Having spent a number of months getting disheartened and frustrated, I bought this book as a last ditch attempt to get my website going before having to pay someone to do it for me. Setting up a website is not something I'd ever done before so I had no technical knowledge at all. Quite simply, this book is superb. It was just like having the web developer sitting next to me at my desk talking me through every little detail. He 'told me' what to ignore (explaining why as he did so), explained what we were doing and why at every step and the pictures aligned to what was on my screen as I went along. Two days later I had a website and now I am actually changing the theme and altering things with confidence. I simply cannot rate this book highly enough. Thank you Andy!" **Louise Burridge**

"Brilliant - all you need to know to get up and running." S. J. Oswald

"I had to design a website urgently and one I could manage myself. I'd read that do this I needed a web design programme that offered CMS, Content Control Management and that Wordpress was the best programme for the job. I was a complete beginner with no knowledge at all about website design. Before I came across Dr Andy Williams book I'd bought two others and became overwhelmed by the complexity and the jargon.

If you want to design your own website, you don't need any other book than this. If you work through it carefully and methodically you'll quickly learn all the technicalities involved and have the vocabulary to create a website that is visually arresting, the content, of course, is up to you.

Dr Williams is a natural-born teacher with that special genius of being able to make a complex process easy and interesting to follow. The large-format book is a pleasure to use. It begins with the assumption that the reader knows nothing about Wordpress, website hosting, registering and costs. The easy to follow steps takes you through this process to the point where once your website is up and running, the reader can download Wordpress, then get to work! Dr Williams takes you through every aspect of the Wordpress 'dashboard,' (the programme's control panel) a place it is important know well, and where the web designer will spend a lot of time. Once the reader is familiar with this, the design process starts and Dr Williams again leads the reader step by step through the website building process.

One of the many outstanding features of the book is the use of screen shots that show the reader what to do and where to do it, it's like using a print out of a video. Another indispensable feature is the "Tasks To Complete" sections found at the end of each major learning phase. The reader is given a list of tasks to work through which consolidates what has been learned, and offers a comprehensive revision structure that can be revisited as many times as necessary.

"The Beginner's Guide to Wordpress" is not just an outstanding book about WordPress, it is also a model of how this kind of "teaching at a distance," should be done. Dr Williams has written several other books using the same teaching techniques, we can only hope the list continues to grow." Dr. Gerald Benedict

DISCLAIMER AND TERMS OF USE AGREEMENT

The author and publisher of this eBook and the accompanying materials have used their best efforts in preparing this eBook. The author and publisher make no representation or warranties with respect to the accuracy, applicability, fitness, or completeness of the contents of this eBook. The information contained in this eBook is strictly for educational purposes. Therefore, if you wish to apply ideas contained in this eBook, you are taking full responsibility for your actions.

The author and publisher disclaim any warranties (express or implied), merchantability, or fitness for any particular purpose. The author and publisher shall in no event be held liable to any party for any direct, indirect, punitive, special, incidental or other consequential damages arising directly or indirectly from any use of this material, which is provided "as is", and without warranties.

The author and publisher do not warrant the performance, effectiveness or applicability of any sites listed or linked to in this eBook.

All links are for information purposes only and are not warranted for content, accuracy or any other implied or explicit purpose.

The author and publisher of this book are not in any way associated with Google.

This eBook is © copyrighted by Dr. Andrew Williams and is protected under the US Copyright Act of 1976 and all other applicable international, federal, state and local laws, with ALL rights reserved. No part of this may be copied, or changed in any format, sold, or used in any way other than what is outlined within this eBook under any circumstances without express permission from Dr. Andrew Williams.

Contents

Who am I & why should you listen to me?

My name is Andy Williams and I am a teacher. In 2001 I gave up teaching in schools where I had been a Science teacher working with students from 11 to 18 years of age. I needed a new challenge, and most of all I wanted to spend more time with my family.

Since then my work (and my hobby), has been to study the search engines and build websites for profit. It's been a long journey and a large number of people have followed me on that passage by reading my free weekly newsletter published over at ezSEONews.com. My newsletter has covered a wide range of topics relevant to webmasters - that's people who own and build their own website(s). If you are interested, you can sign up to receive my free newsletter too.

In the early days, websites were hand-built using a code called Hyper Text Markup Language, or HTML for short. To create good-looking websites, you needed to be something of a geek. Tools like Macromedia Dreamweaver (now owned by Adobe), and Microsoft Front Page (discontinued in 2006), were developed to reduce the coding learning curve associated with building a website in HTML, but these tools were expensive.

Then in May 2003, Matt Mullenweg & Mike Little, released a tool that would change the face of website building forever. They called it WordPress.

I have to admit to being a little reluctant to give up my copy of Dreamweaver, but in 2004 I started to experiment with the WordPress platform. At that time, WordPress was just starting to get interesting with the introduction of "plugins". Don't worry, we'll look at those later in the book, but for now just understand that plugins are an easy and pain-free ways of adding great new functionality to your website.

Fast-forward to today and WordPress is now the site-building tool of choice for many professionals and enthusiasts alike. For example; home businesses run by moms & dads, school kids running blogs about their favorite bands, large corporations, and everyone in between, have all turned to WordPress. It's extremely powerful, flexible, produces very professional looking websites or blogs, is relatively easy to use, and perhaps best of all, it's totally free.

Sure, there is a learning curve, but that is where I come in.

With years of experience teaching technical stuff in an easy to understand manner, I am going to take you by the hand and guide you as you construct your very own professional looking website or blog, even if you know absolutely nothing about how to go about this. The only thing you need to know is how to use a web browser. So if you have ever searched Google for something, then you already have the skills necessary to follow this book.

I have made this book a step-by-step, visual guide to creating your website. Just follow along with the exercises, and in no time at all you'll be using WordPress like a pro as you build a website you can be proud to show your family and friends. In fact, they will probably start asking YOU to help them build their own projects.

Excited?

OK, let's get on with it.

How to Use this Book

I have written this book as a hands-on tutorial. To get the most out of it, I recommend that you sit at your computer, following the steps outlined in its pages. Whenever I do something on my demo site, you then do it on your own site. Don't be afraid of making mistakes; just have fun and experiment with WordPress. Mistakes can easily be undone or deleted, and anyway, most of us learn better by making a few blunders along the way.

By the end of this book you will have a solid understanding of how WordPress works and how you can get it to do what YOU want it to do. If you then decide to take your WordPress knowledge to the next level, you'll have an excellent foundation from which to build upon.

For anyone that likes learning through video, I have a Wordpress video course that you might find interesting. It's got over 8 hours of video tuition, and has a Q&A section so you can ask me questions. The course is hosted on the Udemy platform, and I have a special link for all readers of this book that want to check it out. Using the link below, you can get my Udemy course for just $10:

http://ezseonews.com/wpbook

What is WordPress?

WordPress is a Content Management System (CMS). That just means it is a piece of software that can help you manage and organize your content into an impressive and coherent website.

Initially WordPress was created as a blogging tool, but over the years it has become so much more than that. Today, many WordPress driven sites look nothing like blogs (unless that's what the user wants). This is down to the flexibility of this amazing tool.

WordPress powers simple blogs, corporate websites and everything in between. Companies like Sony, the Wall Street Journal, Samsung, New York Times, Wired, CNN, Forbes, Reuters and many others, all use WordPress as part of their online presence.

WordPress is 'open source', meaning that all of its code is free to use and customize. This is one of the powers of WordPress, since programmers the world over have created their own additions to this powerful publishing platform; from website templates to plugins that extend the functionality of this amazing site building tool.

Some of the features that make WordPress great

• Template system for site design means that changing the look and feel of your site is as simple as installing a new theme - literally just a few clicks of the mouse. There's a plethora of free and quality WordPress themes available.

• Plugins are pieces of code that you can download into your WordPress site to add new features and functions. There are thousands of plugins available and many are totally free.

• Once your site is set up, you can concentrate on adding great content to your site. You simply type into a text editor within the WordPress Dashboard, hit publish, and WordPress takes care of the rest.

• WordPress also has a feature called Widgets that allows the user to drag and drop "features" and place them in, for example, the sidebar. You may have a widget that allows you to display a poll to your visitors - for example. You can place that poll in the sidebar of your site by dragging the poll widget to the appropriate place. Widgets are typically used in the sidebars, but some templates allow widgets to be placed in the site footer as well as on the homepage. We will look at widgets in much more detail later on in this book.

• WordPress can help you with the SEO (Search Engine Optimization), of your site, so that it has the potential to rank better in search engines like Google and BING.

• Wordpress can create just about any type of site, from hobby blog to ecommerce store.

WordPress.com v WordPress.org

There are actually two "flavours" of WordPress. Firstly, there is WordPress from WordPress.com. The second one is WordPress from WordPress.org.

It is vital that you understand the difference between these two.

WordPress.com

WordPress.com allows anyone to sign up for a free WordPress site that WordPress will host on *their* servers. All you need to provide is the content for the site.

Example: Say you wanted to create a website on "educational toys for kids". You could set up a website called educationaltoysforkids.wordpress.com (assuming no one else has taken that name already).

Your website address (URL) would be:

educationaltoysforkids.wordpress.com

.. and by visiting that address in your web browser, you'd see the homepage of your site.

What you actually have is a sub-domain on the wordpress.com domain.

The main downside is that you do not own the site, Wordpress.com do. One day you might go to look at your site and find that it's no longer there. You are playing by their rules.

There is also a number of restrictions on WordPress.com. For example, there are some plugins you won't be able to install and you'll also have a limited choice of themes/templates.

For these reasons, I do not recommend you create your site on WordPress.com. This book will assume you are going to use the other WordPress – the one from WordPress.org.

WordPress.org

WordPress.org is a site where you can download your own copy of WordPress for free. You can then upload that copy of WordPress to any web server you like and start building a site that YOU own. You will also be able to choose whatever domain name you like, so you could call your site educationaltoysforkids.com (if it's available). Doesn't that look more professional than the options on WordPress.com?

Think of the difference between WordPress.com and WordPress.org as being similar to renting or owning a house. When you rent a house, there are limits to what you can do to it. You can be thrown out at any time. When you own the building outright, you can do whatever you want with it and no one can tell you how to design, decorate, or renovate *your* home.

The only disadvantages of using WordPress from WordPress.com are the costs involved. These costs are minimal though, so let's look at them now.

The costs of owning your own site

So how much is a website going to cost you? As you build your site there will be optional costs - things like a website theme, autoresponder or mailing list, but these are totally optional since most things can be done for free. However, there are two costs that you cannot avoid.

The website domain

The website domain is your site's address on the internet. **Google.com** is the website domain of our favourite search engine. **CNN.com** is the domain of a popular international news service.

You will need to buy a domain for your website. We'll look at this later, but for now, let's just consider the price. Typically, a domain name will cost around $10 per year. You can sometimes get the first year for free when you buy web hosting, but once that first year is up, you'll be paying the $10 per year to keep your domain name live.

Your domain name will be registered with a company called a registrar. It is this registrar that will collect the $10 payment every year. The registrar can actually be the same company that you use for your web hosting, or a different company. We'll look at the pros and cons of both options.

Website hosting

Your website needs to be on a computer somewhere that is attached to the internet 24/7 so that people can find it. We call these computers "web servers" and companies that lease, rent or buy them are called web hosts. Their job is to make sure the servers are up, running, and well maintained at all times. You therefore need to rent some disk space on one of these servers to hold your website. We rent server space from a web hosting company. This is a monthly fee of around $5 per month (although it does vary greatly between web hosts).

As mentioned earlier, some web hosts offer a free domain name (for the first year). They can offer a free domain name because you are paying them a monthly fee for the web hosting; therefore, they get their investment back over time. In order to take advantage of the free domain offers, you will need to use your web host as the registrar for your domain.

The total essential costs of running your own website are therefore around $70 per year.

Registrar & web hosts

When you sign up with a web host, you have the choice to let them be the registrar for your website as well. The advantage of this is that all payments you need to make are to the same company, meaning you only have to deal with ONE outfit.

There are disadvantages to this arrangement though, and a lot of people (including myself), prefer to keep host and registrar separate.

Potential problem: If for any reason your web host decides your website is causing them problems (i.e. they get spam complaints, or your website is using up too many system resources), they can take your site down without any warning. What happens next?

Let's look at what happens if you use your web host as registrar.

1. Your site goes down.
2. You contact your host and they tell you that they received spam complaints from your domain.
3. They refuse to put your site back up.
4. You need to move your site to a new host, but your existing host is the registrar and can make that difficult.
5. Your site remains down for a long period of time while you sort things out, and eventually move the site to a new host and registrar.

OK, let's look at what happens if your registrar is separate from your host.

1. Your site goes down.
2. You contact your host and they tell you that they received spam complaints from your domain.
3. They refuse to put your site back up.
4. You order hosting at a new host, and copy your site to the new host.
5. You login to your registrar account and change the name servers (don't worry about this, we'll look at it later), to the new host. This takes seconds to do.
6. Your site is back up within 24 hours or sooner.

This is one scenario where using a separate host and registrar is important.

Another scenario, which doesn't bear thinking about, is if your hosting company goes out of business (it does happen sometimes). So what becomes of your site? Well, you probably lose it AND your domain name if your hosting company is also your registrar.

If your registrar and host are with two separate companies, and this happened, you'd

8

simply get hosting somewhere else and change the name servers at your registrar. With this arrangement, your site would only be down for 24 hours or less.

Another situation that I have heard about is when a hosting company locks you out of your control panel (a login area where you can administer your domain(s)), because of a dispute over something. That means you cannot possibly move the domain to a new host, because you must have access to that control panel to do it. Consequently, your domain will be down for as long as the dispute takes to resolve.

A final word of caution! I have heard horror stories of people not being able to transfer their domain out from a bad webhost. Even worse than that, the domain they registered at the hosting company was not registered in their name, but in the name of the hosting company. I therefore recommend that when you are ready to buy hosting, you consider the web host and registrar that I personally use.

I also recommend that you use a separate registrar and ignore those "free for the first year" offers. However, if you just want the easy option of using one company, use the web host I recommend. I have used them for years (sometimes as a combined host and registrar on a few sites), and never had a problem.

Recommended registrars & webhosts

Since the details (prices, features, etc.), of web hosts in particular, can change so much, I have created a page on my website that list the currently recommended web hosts and registrars.

On that page you'll find out about the features and prices.

Check out my recommended web host and domain registrar:

http://ezseonews.com/dwh

Tasks to complete

1. Sign up for web hosting. If you are going to use a separate registrar, sign up for the registrar first and buy the domain name. Once that is cleared, go and sign up for web hosting and point the domain at your new web server by changing the DNS. Instructions to do this are given on the webpage I mentioned above.

Installing WordPress

For this, you need to login to the cPanel of your hosting. The URL, username and password were all in the welcome email the host sent you when you signed up.

Once you are logged in, scroll down to the **Software** section, and click on the **Softaculous** app installer. Please note that depending on the version of cPanel you are using, your screen may look a little different to mine.

On the next screen, you'll see a box containing the Wordpress logo. Move your mouse over it, and an **Install** button will appear:

Click the **Install** button.

At the top of the next screen, you'll see this:

Software Setup

Choose Protocol

If your site has SSL, then please choose the HTTPS protocol.

http://

Choose Domain

Please choose the domain to install the software.

harlun.co.uk

In Directory

The directory is relative to your domain and **should not exist**. e.g. To install at http://mydomain/dir/ just type **dir**. To install only in http://mydomain/ leave this empty.

wp

In the **"Choose Domain"** box, select the domain where you want to install Wordpress.

In the **"In Directory"** box, delete the pre-filled value, leaving this empty. Failure to delete this will mean your Wordpress website will be installed in that sub-folder (wp in my screenshot). Instead of my website being at harlun.co.uk, it will be at harlun.co.uk/wp. That is NOT what I want, and I guess not what you want, so delete the value and leave it empty.

Next we have these settings:

Site Settings

Site Name

My Blog

Site Description

My WordPress Blog

Enable Multisite (WPMU) ℹ

Enter a name & description for your site. You can change these later, so don't worry too much about it.

Leave Enable Multisite (WPMU) unchecked.

Next we have the Admin account settings:

Admin Account

Admin Username	admin
Admin Password	pass Hide
	Bad (18/100)
Admin Email	admin@harlun.co.uk

Don't use admin as your username. Again, this is the default and makes it easier for hackers. Change your admin username to something else using upper and lower characters, plus numbers. Also add a strong password. You can check how strong your password is with the visual indicator underneath the password box. Use upper and lower characters, numbers and special characters. If you are worried about remembering password, do a Google search for password managers, and use one. They'll remember and fill passwords for you. I personally use one called Roboform.

The username and password combination entered here will be used to login to your Wordpress Dashboard, so make a note of what you enter here.

The "Admin email" box will set the admin email in your Wordpress dashboard, and this will be used to notify you of events, like people leaving comments. This can be changed later.

By default, the language will be set to English, but change this if you need to.

Choose Language

Select Language	English ▾

Softaculous can install a useful plugin for you:

Select Plugins

Limit Login Attempts (Loginizer) ⓘ	☑

Check the box next to **"Limit Login Attempts"**. This is another layer of protection against hackers.

Click the plus sign next to the **"Advanced Options"** title:

■ Advanced Options

Database Name Type the name of the database to be created for the installation	wp669
Table Prefix	wpwp_
Disable Update Notifications ⓘ	☐
Auto Upgrade ⓘ	☐
Auto Upgrade WordPress Plugins ⓘ	☐
Auto Upgrade WordPress Themes ⓘ	☐

The Database Name is set at a random default value. You can change this if you want to. I personally have a lot of databases within my own hosting accounts, so I prefer to use a name that would remind me what the database was being used for. E.g. I might use something like wphar22. The wp prefix would tell me it is a Wordpress site, and "har" would tell me which site. The 22 at the end is just a random couple of digits to make the name more difficult to guess.

The table prefix should also be random. Some Wordpress installation scripts will use wp_ as the default. You absolutely do not want to use that as it makes your site more vulnerable to hackers. Choose something random (Softaculous now does generate a random prefix), so you can use the default one chosen by the installation routine if you want to.

Under these two options, you have some check boxes. These can enable/disable features in your Wordpress installation. You can mouse over the little "I" buttons to see what each option does. I would recommend as a bare minimum that you check "Auto Upgrade". Wordpress will then be automatically updated whenever a new version is released. This helps keep your site more secure. Another useful measure to take is backups, and fortunately, Softaculous offers to take backups for you too:

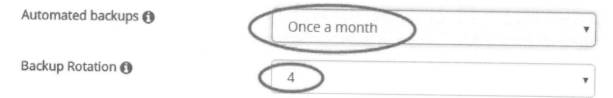

Automated backups ⓘ   Once a month ▾

Backup Rotation ⓘ   4 ▾

In the drop down box for "Automated Backups", select **"Once a Month"** (or more frequently if you will be adding content on a daily basis).

The "Backup Rotation" is the number of backups the host will keep for you. Once that number of backups has been created, the oldest will be deleted to make room for the new backup. On a monthly backup schedule, 4 is about right. If you are backing up more frequently, choose a larger number of backups.

Finally, enter your email address at the bottom before clicking the install button. Your Wordpress login details will be emailed to you at this address when Wordpress is installed.

OK, once the installation has finished, you'll be shown something like this:

Congratulations, the software was installed successfully

WordPress has been successfully installed at :
http://harlun.co.uk/wp
Administrative URL : http://harlun.co.uk/wp/wp-admin/

We hope the installation process was easy.

The first link will load your website (currently a skeleton site created by Wordpress). Here is mine:

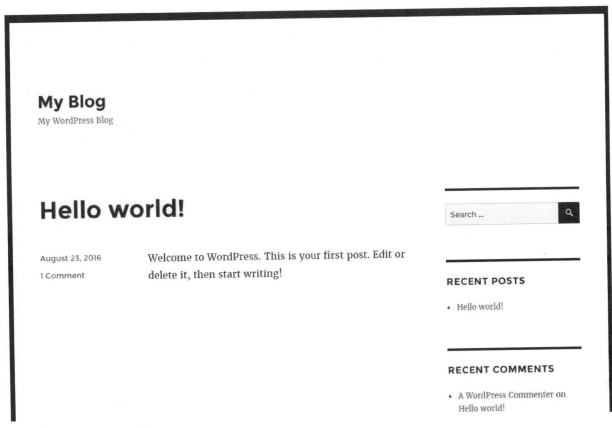

Yours will probably look very similar.

The second URL listed is the Administrative URL. You can click that link to login to the Wordpress Dashboard for your site. The username and password are those that you used when filling in the Admin Details a few minutes ago.

Go check out your site

Go and look at your website in a web browser by typing in the domain URL into the address bar.

You should see your WordPress site up and running. Of course, it won't have any of your content yet and it does come pre-installed with a few pages you'll need to delete, but you should see the homepage displaying a "Hello World!" post.

Before we start learning how to configure the site, let's just login, and then logout again, so we know how.

You should have made a note of the login URL, but if not, just add **/wp-login.php** to the end of your domain name (you can also access the site by adding **/wp-admin** to the end of the URL), e.g.

http://mydomain.com/wp-login.php

or

http://mydomain.com/wp-admin

You'll be taken to the login screen:

Enter the username and password you chose when you were installing WordPress then click the "Log In" button.

I also recommend you check the "Remember Me" box so that your username and password will be automatically entered next time you come to login to your Dashboard.

NOTE: If you ever forget your password, you can click the link under the login boxes to reset your password. The reset instructions will be sent to your admin email address (that's the one you entered when installing WordPress).

After logging in, you will now find yourself inside your Dashboard. You can have a look around but don't go changing anything just yet. Don't worry if it looks a little daunting in there. We'll take a tour of the Dashboard and I'll show you step-by-step, with screenshots, how to set it all up so you can have a great looking website.

NOTE: You will more than likely have notifications that there are some plugins (and even WordPress itself), that need updating. We'll do that in a moment. For now, let's log out so you are clear on how to do that.

Move your mouse over the top right where it says "Howdy Yourname". A menu will appear:

Click the "Log Out" link and you'll be logged out and taken back to the login screen.

Great, WordPress is installed and you now know how to login and logout of your Dashboard.

In the next section we'll take a tour of the Dashboard so you can get your bearings.

Tasks to complete

1. Install WordPress.
2. Login, have a quick look around the Dashboard, then logout again.

The Twenty Sixteen Theme

Wordpress themes define what your site is going to look like. They control the layout, colour, fonts, etc.

Every year or so, Wordpress releases a new default theme. At the time of writing this book, that theme is Twenty Sixteen and next year it is likely to be Twenty Seventeen.

When you install Wordpress, the current default is installed with it, as well as the previous couple of themes. Therefore, as I write this, I can see that Wordpress has installed three themes in my Dashboard. Twenty Sixteen (which is active), Twenty Fifteen and Twenty Fourteen.

In this book, we will keep Twenty Sixteen as the active theme.

To see what themes are installed in your Wordpress Dashboard, look for the **Appearance** menu on the left, and in the popup menu that appears when you hover your mouse over, select **Themes**.

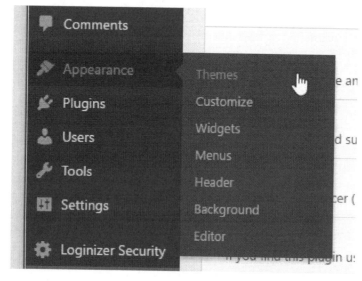

When the page loads, you'll see the installed themes.

I want to delete the Twenty Fifteen and Twenty Fourteen themes as I won't be using them. However, before we do that, would you like to see what they look like?

In the top left of your screen, you will see your website name. Place your mouse pointer over the site name and a menu drops down with one item – **Visit Site**. Click the Visit Site link. This will take you to your website as it appears to anyone that visits.

OK, click the back button on your web browser.

You will go back into the Dashboard for your site, right where you were before clicking on the visit site link.

OK, let's change to another theme.

Put your mouse over one of the other themes installed in your Dashboard and click where it says **Theme Details**. This will open up a screen that displays more information about the theme. At the bottom, you have two buttons and a delete link.

The Activate button will make that theme the new active theme. Go on, try it. Click on Activate. Once activated, click on the Visit Site link again to see what your site looks like. It is very different isn't it? OK; click the back button in your browser to return to the theme page of the Dashboard.

If you have a third theme installed in your Dashboard, check that one out in the same way.

When you've seen the pre-installed themes, make the Twenty Sixteen theme the active theme again. You can take a slight short cut here. Mouse over the Twenty Sixteen theme image and click directly on the **Activate** button. The Twenty Sixteen theme will now become active again. Did you notice the **Live Preview** button? Mouse over an inactive theme and you'll the Live Preview button:

Clicking that button will open up a preview screen showing what your site will look like with that theme, but without actually making it active. You can make it active from that preview screen by clicking the **Save and Activate** button area top left:

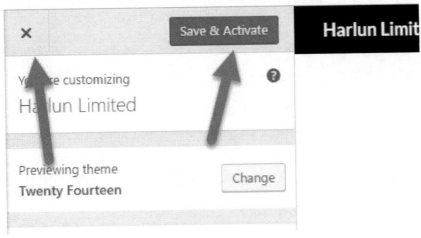

If you just want to close the preview screen without activating the theme, click the **X**.

OK, time to delete the unused themes. This is done for security reasons, as hackers can use old themes (and plugins – see later in the book) as gateways to access your site.

You can probably guess how to do this. Move your mouse over the theme you want to delete, and click the **Theme Details** button. Click the **Delete** link on the details page. You will be asked for confirmation to delete.

Repeat the process to delete all non-active themes. You should only be left with one at the end – Twenty Sixteen.

Whoops, I've Deleted Twenty Sixteen

There may be a time when you need to install a theme. For example, if you buy this book in the future and Twenty Sixteen is not installed by default and you want to follow along with the book. Or maybe you accidentally deleted Twenty Sixteen. The good news is that you can easily install a theme from within your Dashboard.

First thing to do is click on the **Themes** menu inside the **Appearance** menu. This is the screen we've been on in the previous section of this chapter. At the top, you should see an **Add New** button. Click it.

You will see an **Add New** button at the top. Click it.

The Add Themes screen has a search box along the top to help you find themes. Enter Twenty Sixteen. As you do, you will notice the search results automatically update. The Twenty Sixteen theme should appear.

If you don't already have it installed, you can mouse over the theme image and click the install button:

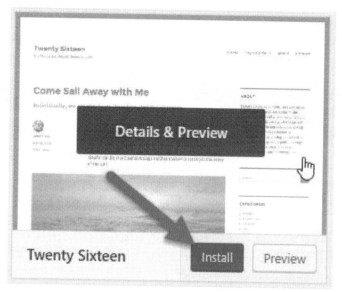

If you already have the theme installed, the image of the theme will have the word installed written across the top.

Before you leave this section, make sure that you have set the Twenty Sixteen theme as active, and deleted all other themes.

In the next chapter, we are going to have a look around the Wordpress Dashboard.

An overview of the Dashboard

When you login to WordPress, you are presented with the Dashboard. This is what it looks like:

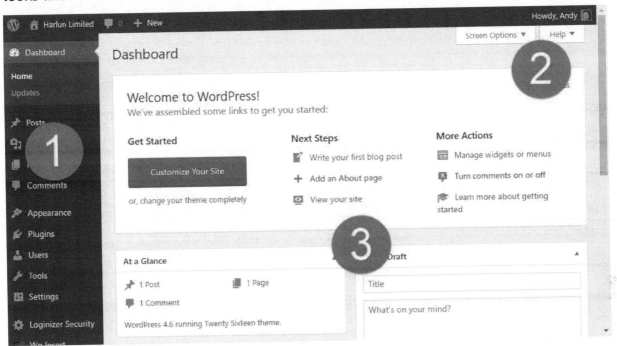

1. The Sidebar
2. Screen Options, Help, Profile & Logout
3. The Main screen

Let's look at each of these in turn.

The sidebar

The sidebar is the main navigation system of your Dashboard. From the sidebar, you can set up your website to look and behave as you want it to. This is where you can add/edit content on your site, upload images, moderate comments, change your site theme, add/remove plugins, and everything else you will need to do as a website owner. We'll look at all of these features in detail later in the tutorial.

Screen options, help, profile & logout

Screen Options is a drop down menu that allows you decide what is shown on the various screens within the Dashboard. If you click the Screen Options link you'll see something like this:

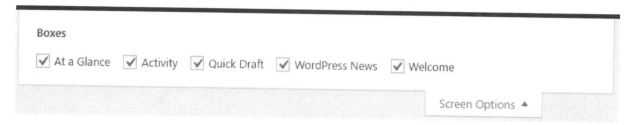

What you see will depend on where you are in the dashboard (and what version of Wordpress you are using), because the options that are shown are relevant to the current page you are viewing. For example, if you are in section for moderating comments, the screen options you will see will be relevant to commenting.

By changing the options in these **Screen Options**, you can change what is displayed in your Dashboard. If you don't want to see something you simply uncheck it.

If you are following this book, or any Wordpress tutorial, and you find that something is missing from the screen that should be there, go in and check the screen options to ensure that it's enabled. We will be popping into the screen options a few times in this book.

To the right of the Screen options button is a button to access WordPress help. Clicking it opens up a help panel:

Overview	Welcome to your WordPress Dashboard! This is the screen you will see when you log in to your site, and gives you access to all the site management features of WordPress. You can get help for any screen by clicking the Help tab in the upper corner.	For more information:
Navigation		Documentation on Dashboard
Layout		
Content		Support Forums

Help ▲

 Dashboard

The left side of this help panel is tabbed, offering you categorized help sections. Like the screen options, the help panel in context-sensitive, so will show you the most useful help items for the Dashboard area you are currently working in.

If you need more detailed help, there are links on the right side which point to the WordPress support forums and more Dashboard documentation.

Finally, in this area of the Dashboard screen, if you place your mouse over the "Howdy Yourname" top right, a panel opens up:

NOTE: Mine shows a photo of myself. I'll show you how & why later when we look at Gravatars in the User Profile section.

This section of the Dashboard gives you a direct link to your profile (which we will fill out later), and a link to logout of your WordPress Dashboard. Whenever you finish a session in the WordPress Dashboard, it's always a good idea to log out.

The main screen

This is where all of the work takes place. What you see in the main screen area will depend on where you are in the Dashboard. For example, if you are in the comments section, the main screen area will list all the comments people have made on your site. If you are in the appearance section of your Dashboard, the main screen section will show you the theme/template of your site. If you are adding or editing a post, the main screen area will have everything you need to add/edit a post.

Tasks to complete

1. Go in and explore the Dashboard to familiarize yourself with the system.
2. Go and check out the pre-installed Wordpress Themes.
3. Delete all inactive themes, for security reasons. You should be left with just the Twenty Sixteen theme.

23

4. Click on a few of the menu items in the left navigation column and then open the screen options to see what it contains. See how the options are related to the page you are viewing in the Dashboard?

5. Have a look at the help options – the forum and the other WordPress documentation. You won't need any of that now, but it is a good idea to be familiar with these options just in case you get stuck in the future.

Cleaning out the preinstalled stuff

When you install WordPress, it installs a few default items like the "Hello World" post you saw on the homepage earlier. In addition to that post, there is a "Sample page", a comment, some widgets and a few plugins.

NOTE: WordPress allows you to create two types of content – posts and pages. Don't worry about the differences between these just yet as we'll look at them later.

In this chapter, we'll look at deleting the pre-installed post, comment, page and widgets. We'll leave the plugins for later in this book.

Deleting the "Hello World" post

This is the first thing we need to delete. If you visit your site homepage right now - before deleting it - you'll see that the "Hello World" post is displayed front and centre.

To delete the post, we need to open the "Posts" menu from the left hand sidebar navigation.

To do this you can either move your mouse over the word **Posts**, and select **All Posts** from the popup menu, like this:

Or you can click the word **Posts**, and the sub-menu will become integrated into the left sidebar. You can then click the **All Posts** link:

This will open up a table of all posts on your site:

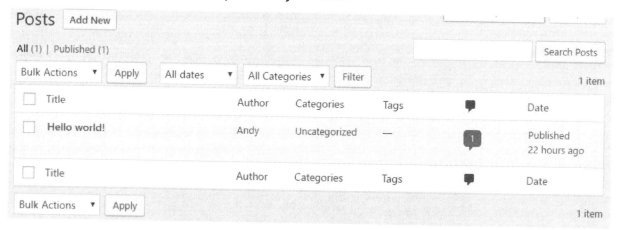

Something to try...

Open up the **Screen Options** top right, and uncheck/check some of the boxes to see how it affects what you see on your screen.

Try out the **Excerpt View** in the **View Mode** Section (hint: You will need to click the Apply button for that to take effect).

OK; now you've had some fun, let's delete the Hello World post.

Move your mouse over the title of the post. A menu appears underneath:

This menu allows you to:

1. Edit the post
2. Quick Edit - which allows you to edit title, category, etc., but not the content of the post.
3. Move the post to Trash (i.e. delete it).
4. View the post – which will open the post in the current browser window.

We want to delete the post, so click on the "Trash" link. The screen will refresh and the post will be gone.

If you accidentally delete a post, don't worry. It will remain in the trash until you empty the trash. I actually want to keep the "Hello World!" post on my site so that I can use it later in the book. Let's undelete the post.

To do this, you go to the **All Posts** screen (which is where we are right now), and look for the **Trash** link above the tables of posts.

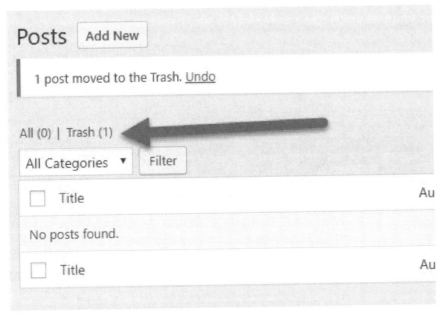

There is a (1) next to the Trash link. That means there is one item in the trash (my Hello Word post). If you click on the Trash link, you'll be taken to the trash bin where you can see all of the posts that were sent to there.

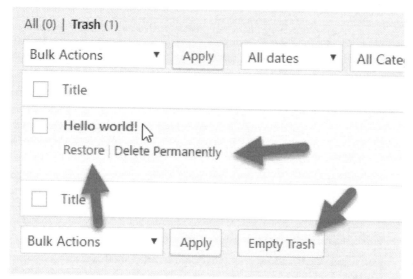

If you mouse-over the post title, you'll get another popup menu. This one allows you to restore the post (i.e. undelete it), or delete it permanently.

If you have a lot of posts in the trash and you want to delete them all, click the "Empty Trash" button at the bottom.

NOTE: When WordPress created the "Hello World!" post, it also added a demo comment to the post. When you deleted the post, the comment was also deleted because it belonged to that post. When you undelete (restore) a post, any comments that were deleted with the post are also restored.

I am going to click on the **Restore** link to restore the Hello World post and comment. You can do the same if you wish. You know how to delete it when you decide you want to.

Deleting the sample page

In the sidebar navigation of your Dashboard, open the **Pages** menu and click on **All Pages**.

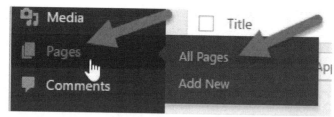

Like the posts section, this will bring up a list of all pages on the site. Mouse over the Sample page title, and click the **Trash** link underneath it.

As with posts, pages remain in the trash until it's emptied and can therefore be restored it required.

Deleting widgets

WordPress pre-configured your website with a number of widgets in the sidebar of your website. You can see them if you look at your website:

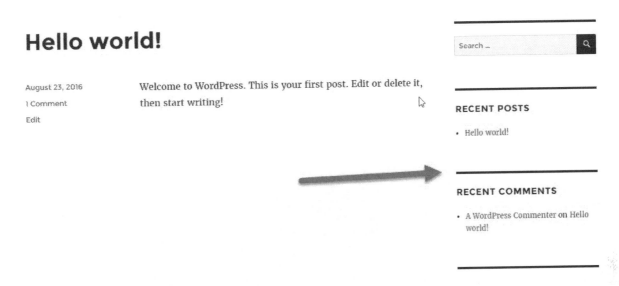

Those are widgets on the right. Let's delete them.

In your Dashboard, move your mouse over the **Appearance** menu, and click on **Widgets**:

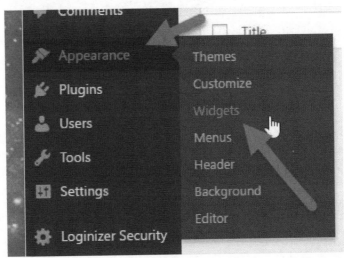

This will take you to the widget screen:

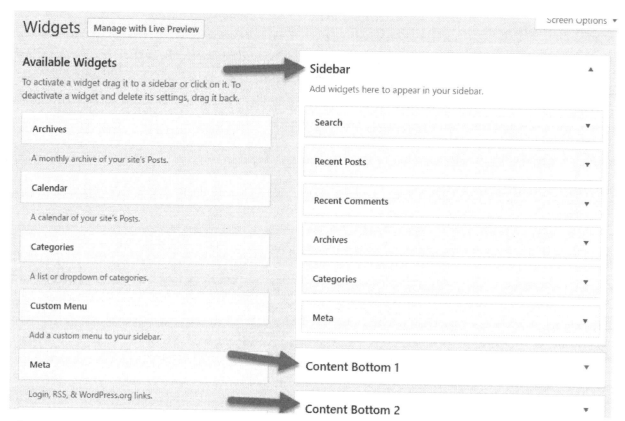

The screen is split into two sections.

On the left you'll see the **Available widgets**.

On the right, you have "widgetized areas". These are areas on your web page that can hold widgets. For example, the top widgetized area is the Sidebar (this section is opened in my screenshot to show 6 widgets in the sidebar area). Any widgets in this area will appear in the sidebar on the website.

You can insert widgets into the widgetized areas of your site by dragging and dropping them onto the corresponding area on the right. Be aware that different templates have different widgetized areas, so if you are not using the Twenty Sixteen theme from Wordpress, you will be seeing something a little different on the right hand side.

The Twenty Sixteen theme also has two other widgetized areas called **Content Bottom 1** and **Content Bottom 2**. These correspond to areas on your web page, but where?

The easiest way to find out is to drag a widget into each area and see where they appear on the Hello World post.

Click and drag a Calendar Widget into the Content Bottom 1 widgetized area. Drop it there. Under the title for the widget, type Content Bottom 1.

In the Content Bottom 2 area, drag and drop a Text widget. When you drop it, there is space for you to add a title and the content. Fill it in with something. Here is mine:

Content Bottom 2

Appears at the bottom of the content on posts and pages.

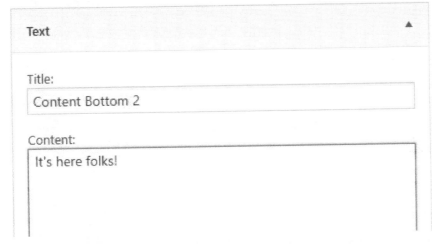

Once you've typed something in, click the Save button at the bottom of the text widget.

OK; now go and visit your website.

You won't see the calendar or text widget on the homepage. We need to visit a post (don't worry, this will all

become clear later in the book). To visit the Hello World post, click on the Hello World title on your homepage. As you move your mouse over the title, it should change colour (indicating it is a link). After clicking the title, you'll land on the Hello World post, and if you scroll down, you will see the Content Bottom 1 & 2 widgetized areas at the bottom of the screen (after the post and comments section).

CONTENT BOTTOM 1

August 2016

M	T	W	T	F	S	S
1	2	3	4	5	6	7
8	9	10	11	12	13	14
15	16	17	18	19	20	21
22	23	24	25	26	27	28
29	30	31				

CONTENT BOTTOM 2

It's here folks!

So widgetized areas are simply pre-defined areas on your webpage that allows you to insert something (in the form of a widget).

All WordPress themes are different and will provide you with their own unique widgetized areas. Common areas include the footer, sidebar and even header of the web page. The best way to find out where each widgetized area is on the website is to consult the documentation that came with your theme or just add a widget and see where it appears.

OK; let's clear out the pre-installed widgets, and those two we just added.

WordPress installed several widgets into the "Main Sidebar" area of your site.

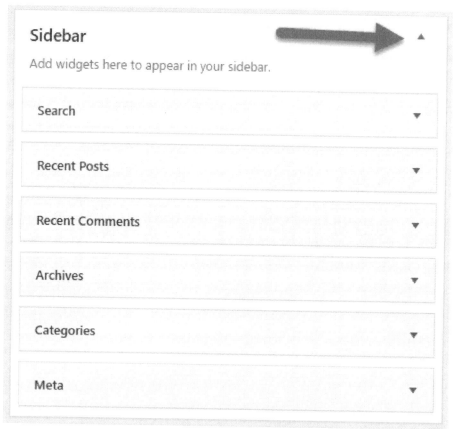

You can open up each widgetized area using the arrow to the right of the area title.

In the sidebar, you can see widgets called Search, recent posts, recent comments, archives, categories and Meta.

Each installed Widget has a small downward-pointing arrow next to it on the right. Click this arrow to open up the settings for that particular widget:

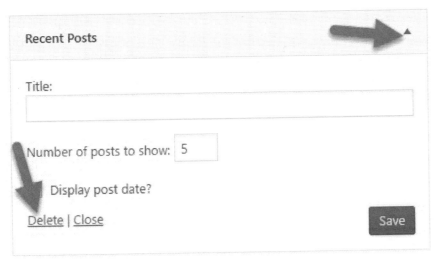

You'll see that there are a couple of options available for this "Recent Posts" widget. You can enter a title (leaving this blank will use the default title for the widget, in this case "Recent Posts"). You can also specify how many posts to show. This one is set to 5.

To delete the widget, click the **Delete** link bottom left.

The widget will disappear from the Main Sidebar area. Repeat to delete all of the other widgets in the sidebar (and the two we added to the other areas). The only one I am leaving for now is the **Meta** widget. This gives me an easy link to login to my site from the homepage, so I'll keep it there for now while I am working on the site. You can do the same if you wish.

OK, we are done cleaning out WordPress.

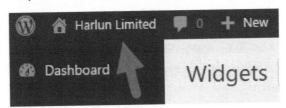

Click the link to your homepage (top left of the dashboard) to see what your site now looks like:

Harlun Limited
Company Website

Hello world!

August 23, 2016

1 Comment

Edit

Welcome to WordPress. This is your first post. Edit or delete it, then start writing!

META

- Site Admin
- Log out
- Entries RSS
- Comments RSS
- WordPress.org

Harlun Limited / Proudly powered by WordPress

If you deleted the Hello World post, you will just see a message saying "Nothing Found". In my screenshot, the Hello World post is shown on the homepage, and you can see the Meta widget I left in the right sidebar.

Tasks to complete

1. Delete the Hello World post and then go into the trash and restore it.
2. Delete the pre-installed Page.
3. Explore the various widgets that Wordpress has given you. Drag & drop then into widgetized areas to see what they look like on your website, and where they appear. Note that some widgets may show nothing at all. This is simply because there is nothing to show until there is some data they can work with.

Dashboard updates

WordPress makes it easy for us to know when there are updates. At the top of the screen, you'll see a notification whenever there is a new update to WordPress itself.

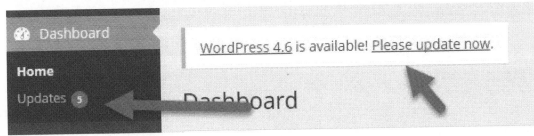

You'll also see a number 5 in a circle next to the Updates menu (which is inside the main Dashboard menu). That number 5 means that there are 5 updates waiting to be installed. The screenshot above is taken from an established site of mine. These 5 updates include various plugins I use on that site. You won't have any yet, but I wanted to show you what it looked like.

We can find all available updates in the "Updates" section. Just click it in the menu:

At the top of that screen, there will be a section for WordPress updates (if there is one available):

To update WordPress to the latest version, simply click the "Update Now" button and follow the onscreen instructions.

Occasionally these WordPress updates will require you to click a button or two, e.g. to update the database:

Just follow all screen prompts, and the update will complete and take you back to the Dashboard.

If I once again go to the **Updates** screen, I am now told Wordpress is up-to-date. However, underneath that, there are plugins that need updating:

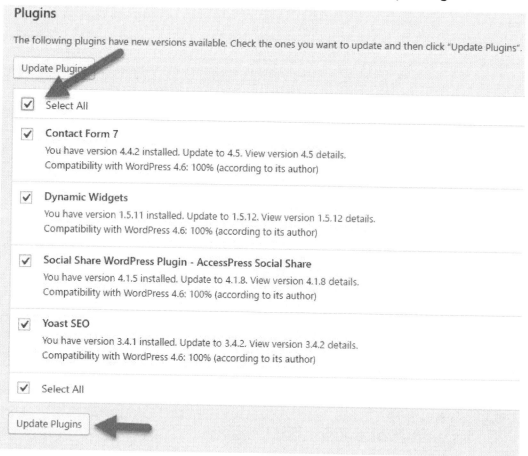

You can update all plugins by checking the box next to each one (the **Select All** checkbox will check them all with a single click), and then clicking the **Update Plugins** button.

Once the plugin updates have been completed, WordPress will ask you where you want to go next:

All updates have been completed.

Return to Plugins page | Return to WordPress Updates page

If there are still updates to perform, click the link to return to WordPress updates.

With all updates now complete, we can actually go anywhere we want by clicking the relevant option in the Dashboard's navigation sidebar.

OK, let's configure WordPress so that it is ready for our content.

Tasks to complete

1. Check to see if there are any updates waiting for your installation of Wordpress. If there are, go and update everything. Whenever you login to you Dashboard, if there are updates pending, it is a good idea (for security reasons) to update them immediately.

WordPress Settings

In the sidebar navigation of your Dashboard, you'll see an item labeled **Settings**.

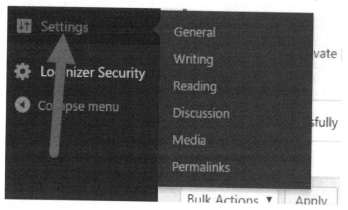

Within **Settings** we have a number of items. Let's look at each one in turn and configure things as we go through.

General Settings

The General settings page defines some of the basic website settings.

At the top of the screen, the first few settings look like this:

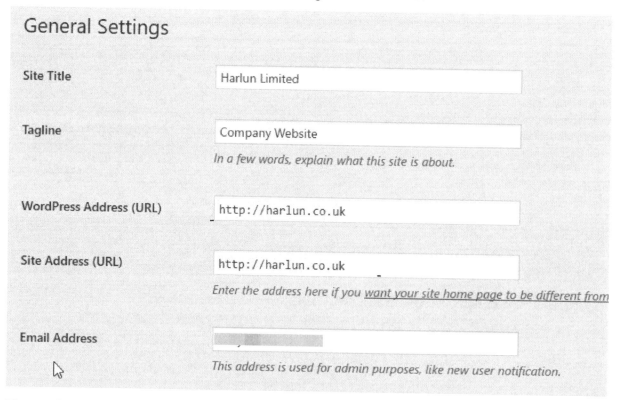

The information on the General Settings page was filled in when you installed WordPress, and there is probably no reason to change anything.

Right at the top is the Site Title. This is usually the same as the domain name, but doesn't have to be.

Under the title is the Tagline. On some themes the tagline is displayed in the site header right under the site name. The Twenty Sixteen theme is one theme that does this. Go and check out your website and you'll see the tagline sitting right underneath he site title.

You typically use the tagline to give your visitors a little bit more information about your website. A tagline may be your website's "catch phrase", slogan, mission statement, or just a very brief, one sentence description.

The next two fields on this settings page are the **WordPress Address (URL)** and the **Site Address (URL)**. The WordPress Address is the URL where WordPress is installed. Since we installed it in the root folder of this site, the WordPress Address is identical to the Website Address.

NOTE: Advanced users might want to install WordPress in a folder on their site, yet still have the WordPress site appear as if it were in the root folder. They can achieve this by using the WordPress Address (URL) field. Confused? Don't be. You won't be doing this.

Next on this setting page is the email address. This is very important as you'll get all notifications sent to this email address. Make sure you use a valid email that you actually check frequently. Later in the book we'll assign a Gravatar to this email address and set up a backup system that sends you an email backup of your WordPress database at set intervals.

Lower down this General Setting page are some more options:

Membership	☐ Anyone can register
New User Default Role	Subscriber ▼

The **Membership** option allows visitors to sign up on your site, with their role being defined in the **New User Default Role** drop down box. E.g. you could allow visitors to sign up as subscribers or maybe contributors. However, this can open up a whole can of security worms, so I don't advise you enable this option. If you want to create a "membership" site, use a dedicated, secure Wordpress membership plugin like Wishlist Member (which can turn any Wordpress site into a fully-fledged membership site).

The rest of the settings on this page allow you to set your time zone, date and time formats.

The time zone is used to correctly timestamp posts on your site. Since we'll look at how you can schedule your posts into the future, the correct time zone will ensure your posts are going out at the intended dates and times.

Select the date and time format you use.

You can also set the day you use for the start of the week. This will be used if you use a calendar widget in your sidebar. If you choose Monday as the start of the week, then Monday will be the first column in the calendar.

If you make any changes to the settings on the General Settings tab, make sure you save the changes when you are finished.

Writing

The writing settings control the user interface you see when you are adding/editing posts. Let's look at the options.

Here are the first two:

The **Default Post Category** is the category that a post will be assigned to if you don't manually select a category. We haven't set up any categories yet. Wordpress set one up for us during installation, called **Uncategorized**, so that is the current default. We'll rename that to something more useful when we look at categories later in the course.

The **Default Post Format** is the default layout/appearance of the posts you add to your site. This is controlled by the template you are using, with different templates having different options. Here are the post formats in Twenty Sixteen:

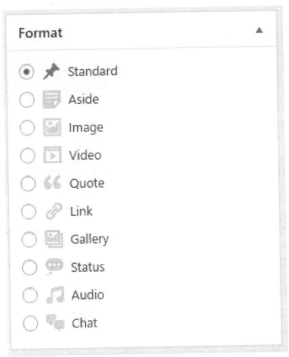

Each of these will modify how the posts look, so I recommend you use the Standard option for the default value, and then change the format on a post by post basis if needed. We'll see how to do that later.

Here are the next few settings:

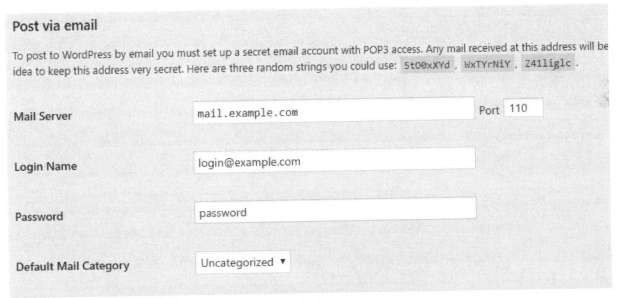

The Post via e-mail can be set up so that you can post content to your site by sending it in as an email. This is beyond the scope of this book.

The final setting on this page IS important. It's the update services:

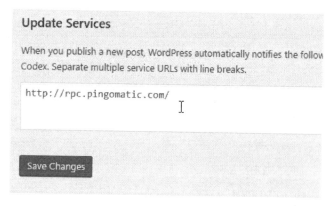

Basically, every time you post new content on your site, a message is sent to all services in this list (currently just one) to let them know there is new content. They will then typically come over to your site to index the content.

This helps get your content noticed by, and included in, the search engines a lot faster. WordPress installs just one service, but I recommend you add more.

Do a search of Google for "WordPress Ping List" and you'll find people have created lists of services you can add. Just find a list and paste it into the box. Save your changes before moving to the next settings page.

Reading

The reading settings define how your visitors will see certain aspects of your site.

There are only a few settings here, but they are important.

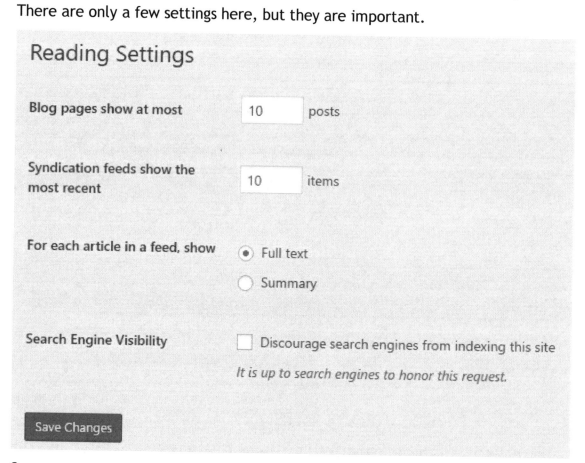

Some pages on your site like the category, tag and home page can show lists of posts.

Blog pages show at most, defines how many posts appear on those page.

This setting will make more sense when you start adding content to your site. You'll then be able to see what WordPress does with that content as you add it.

Here is an example. If you have a category on your site called "types of roses", then WordPress will create a category page called "Types of Roses" that lists all of the posts in that category. If you have 15 articles, each describing a different rose, then WordPress will create two category pages to hold those articles (assuming you left the default set to 10 per page). The first category page will have links to the first 10, and the second will list the remaining 5.

I recommend you leave the setting at the default 10.

Syndication feeds show the most recent, refers to your website's RSS feed. Every WordPress site has an RSS feed (in fact it has many RSS feeds). An RSS feed is just a list of the most recent articles with a link and a description for each post. This particular setting allows you to define how many of your most recent posts appear in the feed. Again, I recommend 10. We'll look at RSS feeds in more detail later on.

For each article in a feed, show, defines what content is shown in the feed. If you select "Full Text", then the complete articles are included in the feed. This can make your feed very long, but also give spammers a chance to steal your content with tools designed to scrape RSS feeds and post the content to their own sites.

I recommend you change this setting to Summary. That way only a short summary of each post will be displayed in the feed, which is far less appealing to spammers and easier on the eye for those who genuinely follow your active RSS feeds.

Search Engine Visibility allows you to effectively turn off the site from the search engines. If you are working on a site that you don't yet want the search engines to spider and index, you can check this box.

I actually allow search engines to visit and index my site from day 1. Yes, the search engines will find content that is not finished, but that's OK because they'll come back and check the site periodically to pick up changes.

Whether you block the search engines now or not is up to you. Just remember that if you do, your site won't start appearing in the search engines until you unblock them.

I recommend you leave this setting unchecked.

Make sure you click the **Save Changes** button at the bottom if you've edited the settings on the screen.

NOTE: If you have created a WordPress Page on your site, there will be another section added to the top of this screen that allows you to define what content is shown on your homepage. The section looks like this:

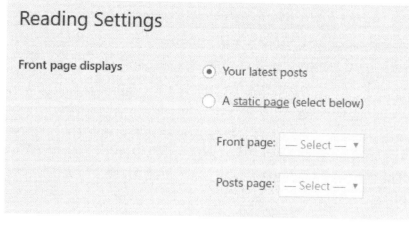

Reading Settings

Front page displays

- ● Your latest posts
- ○ A static page (select below)

Front page: — Select — ▾

Posts page: — Select — ▾

The default setting is **Your Latest Posts**. This will display the most recent posts on your homepage. The number of posts displayed on your homepage is determined by whatever you have the **Blog pages show at most** set to. Since the default is 10, that means your last 10 posts will appear on your homepage.

However, it is possible to set up the homepage like a more traditional website, with a single article forming the basis of the homepage content. You can do this in WordPress by creating a WordPress PAGE that contains your homepage article. You then select **A Static Page** from the options and choose the page from the **Front Page** drop down list. We'll do this later.

Discussion

The discussion settings are related to comments that visitors may leave at the end of your posts. There are a few settings we need to change from the default.

Here are the first few settings in the discussion options:

Default article settings

- ☑ Attempt to notify any blogs linked to from the article
- ☑ Allow link notifications from other blogs (pingbacks and trackbacks) on new articles
- ☑ Allow people to post comments on new articles

(These settings may be overridden for Individual articles.)

Attempt to notify any blogs linked to from the article should be left checked. Whenever you write an article and link to another site, WordPress will try to notify that site that you have linked to them. WordPress does this by sending what is called a Ping. Pings will show up in the comment system of the receiving blog and can be approved like a comment. If it is approved, that Pingback will appear near the comments section on that blog, giving you a link back to your site.

NOTE: Any website can turn pingbacks off. If a ping is sent to a site where pingbacks are OFF, then it won't appear in their comment system.

Here are some example pingbacks published on a web page:

3 Responses to *Men's Health Week Proclamations*

1. Pingback: health » Blog Archive » Focus on Men's Health Week This Father's Day : Healthymagination

2. Pingback: Focus on Men's Health Week This Father's Day : Healthymagination – health

3. Pingback: Focus on Men's Health Week This Father's Day : Healthymagination – men health

Each pingback is a link back to a website that has linked to this webpage.

The next option - **Allow link notifications from other blogs (pingbacks and trackbacks)** allows you to turn pingbacks and trackbacks (trackbacks are very similar to pingbacks) off. If you uncheck this, you will not receive pingbacks or trackbacks.

Should you check it or not?

Well, it's always nice to see when a site is linking to your content. However, there is a technique used by spammers to send fake trackbacks & pingbacks to your site. They are trying to get you to approve their trackback so that your site will then link to theirs.

Personally I uncheck this option, but if you do leave it checked, then never approve a trackback or pingback. They are nearly always spam!

Allow people to post comments on new articles should remain checked. It is important that you let your visitors comment on your site's content. A lot of people disable this because they think moderating comments it too much work, but from an SEO point of view, search engines love to see active discussions on websites. Leave it checked!

The next section of options is shown below:

Other comment settings	
☑	Comment author must fill out name and email
☐	Users must be registered and logged in to comment
☐	Automatically close comments on articles older than `14` days
☑	Enable threaded (nested) comments `5 ▼` levels deep
☐	Break comments into pages with `50` top level comments per page and the `last ▼` page displayed by default
	Comments should be displayed with the `older ▼` comments at the top of each page

Leave all of these at their default value (shown above).

The options are fairly self-explanatory but let's go through them quickly.

The first option requires commenters to fill in a name and email. This is very important and often a good indicator of legitimate/spam comments. Spammers tend to fill the name field with keywords (for SEO purposes), whereas legitimate commenters are more likely to use a real name. The email is nice too, so you can follow up with commenters.

The second item should definitely remain unchecked, because we do not allow visitors to register and login to our site. We do want *all* visitors to have the option of leaving a comment though.

The third option allows you to close the comment sections on posts after a certain number of days. I like to leave comments open indefinitely as you never know when someone will find your article and want to have their say. However, if you want to cut back on spam comments, then close comments after a reasonable length of time, say 30 days.

Nested comments should be enabled. This allows people to engage in discussions within the comments section, with replies to previous comments appearing "nested" underneath the comment they are replying to. Here is an example showing how nested comments appear on my site:

Marshall says:

18/6/2013 at 06:06

I purchased the KD Suite tonight because Andy does good videos. I could have purchased directly from Guindon since I had purchased other products from him. However the productpay.com fulfillment system absolutely sucks. I did not get my bonus downloads because the bonus page got closed before I could get all the membership BS set up and then back to the download page. As opposed to other systems such as JVZoo where you get download information and login information from them, productpay sucks your money and does not much else. And they have no way to contact them without setting up another account with them just to send a support ticket. Plus they hide behind Domains by Proxy owned by Godaddy.com. What kind of legitimate fulfillment company needs to hide their registration information. I have contacted Guindon directly about this and I am sure Dave will make it right. But what a pain in the butt process. If you purchase from productpay.com just be forwarned to download everything first then worry about any membership BS.

You can bet none of Dr Andy's membership sites worked like this. I know because I bought a lot of his products.

Reply

Andy Williams says:

18/6/2013 at 07:59

Totally agree Marshall. They really could do a lot better. Also, thanks for your loyalty 😊

Reply

Marshall says:

18/6/2013 at 09:56

Andy You are welcome. Your software has always worked out of the box without a lot of bugs. And the very few that came up you fixed right away. Your courses were right on the mark too. For what it is worth, Dave got about 5 emails from me tonight so maybe he will rethink his choice of fulfillment companies.

The KD Bestseller analyzer was worth the hassle of getting it and getting it activated. I have played with it for about 3 hours tonight. My niche I was writing in is a real loser for making money. The fiction, adventure, romance are really hot now. I have one more herb book to do

You can see that replies to the previous comment are nested underneath them, making it clear that the comments are part of a conversation.

The last two options in this section relate to how comments are displayed on the page. If you want, comments can be spread across multiple pages, with say 50 comments per page (default). However, I leave this option unchecked so that all comments for an article appear on the same page. If you find that you get hundreds of comments per article, you might like to enable this option just so pages load a lot quicker.

The final option in this section allows you to show older or newer comments at the top of the comments section.

I prefer to have comments listed in the order in which they are submitted as that makes more sense. Therefore, leave the setting as "older".

The next section of these settings is shown below:

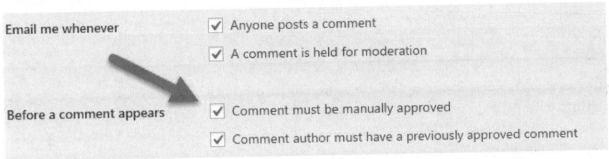

The first two options will send you an email whenever someone posts a comment, and when a comment is held for moderation. We'll actually set up comments so that ALL comments must be moderated so the second option is less important.

Leave both of the first two options checked so that you know when someone leaves a comment. When you get an email notification, you can then login to your Dashboard and either approve the comment (so it goes live on your site), or send it to trash if it's blatant spam.

The second two options shown above relate to when a comment can appear on the site. Check the box next to **Comment must be manually approved**. This will mean ALL comments must be approved by you. We don't want spammy comments appearing on the site and since they'll only appear when we approve them, we have 100% control.

Since we are now moderating all comments, the **Comment author must have a previously approved comment** is not important. What this setting can do is auto-approve comments for any author that has a previously approved comment on the site. For this to work, the previous option should remain unchecked.

I don't advise this you enable this feature. A particular hacking technique (zero-day exploit) targeted sites that were setup to auto-approve comments once a first comment was approved. Hackers would get a harmless comment approved, and then post a comment that contained malicious JavaScript. The JavaScript comment would never have been manually approved, but with their first comment already approved, it would get automatic approval.

Set up your settings as I have them in the screenshot above.

The comment moderation settings are not important to us since all our comments are moderated.

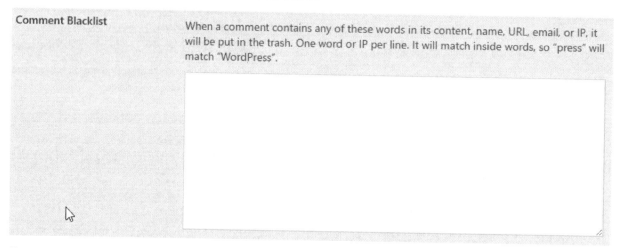

If you do not have it set up to moderate all comments, you can use this setting to automatically add comments to the moderation queue IF it has a certain number of links in it (default is 2), OR the comment contains a word that is listed in the big box.

Since all of our comments are moderated anyway, we can leave this section as it is.

The Comment Blacklist box allows you to set up a blacklist to automatically reject comments that meet the criteria listed here.

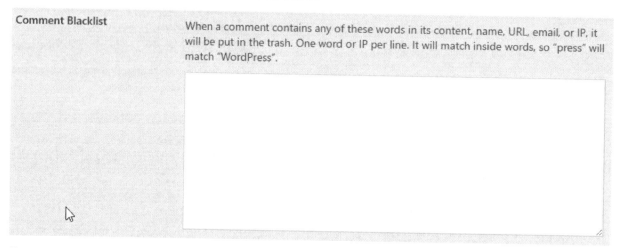

Essentially any comment that contains a word or URL listed in this box, or comes from an email address or IP address listed in this box, will automatically be sent to the trash.

That means you can set up your blacklist with "unsavory" words, email addresses, URLs or IP addresses of known spammers, and you'll never see those comments in your moderation queue. The comment blacklist can significantly cut down on your comment moderation, so I suggest you do a search on Google for **WordPress comment blacklist**, and use a list that someone else has already put together (you'll find a few). Just copy and paste their list into the box and save the settings.

The final section of the discussion options is related to Avatars:

Avatars

An avatar is an image that follows you from weblog to weblog appearing beside your name when you comment on ava Here you can enable the display of avatars for people who comment on your site.

Avatar Display	☑ Show Avatars
Maximum Rating	⦿ G — Suitable for all audiences
	○ PG — Possibly offensive, usually for audiences 13 and above
	○ R — Intended for adult audiences above 17
	○ X — Even more mature than above

An Avatar is a little graphic that appears next to the commenter's name.

I think it is nice to see who is leaving comments, so I recommend you leave Avatars on (first setting).

For most websites you should have the maximum rating set to G. This will then hide any Avatars that are not suitable for your viewers. Avatars are assigned ratings when you create them over at Gravatar.com, so this ratings system is only as good as the honesty of the person creating the avatar.

The final setting allows you to define the default action if someone does not have an Avatar set up for their email address.

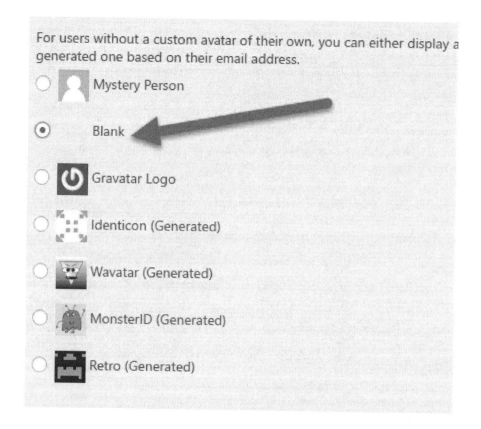

I recommend you select **Blank** so that no avatar is shown. This is because Avatar images need to load with the page. Any page with a lot of comments will have a lot of Avatars to load and this slows down the load speed of the page. Why slow it further with "Mystery Man" avatars (the default setting) when the commenter doesn't have an avatar set up?

When you have finished with these settings, save the changes you made.

Media

The media settings relate to images and other media that you might insert into your site.

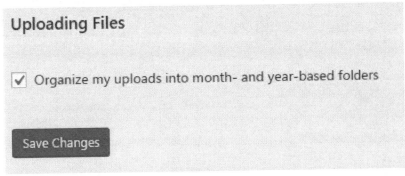

Image sizes

The sizes listed below determine the maximum dimensions in pixels to use when adding an image to the

Thumbnail size   Width [150]   Height [150]

☑ Crop thumbnail to exact dimensions (normally thumbnail

Medium size   Max Width [300]   Max Height [300]

Large size   Max Width [1024]   Max Height [1024]

These first few settings allow you define the maximum dimensions for thumbnail, medium and large images. You can leave these are the default setting.

The final option asks whether you want your uploaded images to be organized into month and year based folders.

Uploading Files

☑ Organize my uploads into month- and year-based folders

[Save Changes]

I'd recommend you leave this checked, just so your images are organized into dates on your server. It can help you find the images later if you need to.

Permalinks

The final settings are the permalinks. Basically these define how the URLs (web address), are constructed for content on your site. This needs to be changed from the default value.

We want the URLs on our site to help visitors and search engines, so we'll add in the post's category and name to the URL:

Common Settings

○ Plain   `http://harlun.co.uk/?p=123`

○ Day and name   `http://harlun.co.uk/2016/08/24/sample-post/`

○ Month and name   `http://harlun.co.uk/2016/08/sample-post/`

○ Numeric   `http://harlun.co.uk/archives/123`

○ Post name   `http://harlun.co.uk/sample-post/`

⦿ Custom Structure   `http://harlun.co.uk` `/%category%/%postname%/`

Select the **Custom Structure** radio button at the bottom of the list, and enter the following into the box:

/%category%/%postname%/

Save the changes.

The URLs on your site will now look like this:

http://mydomain/category/post-name

The last two options on this settings page are shown below:

Optional

If you like, you may enter custom structures for your category and tag URLs here. For example, using t⌐ would make your category links like `http://harlun.co.uk/topics/uncategorized/` . If you leave t⌐ used.

Category base

Tag base

Save Changes

I would leave these two boxes empty.

When WordPress creates a category page or a tag page, the URL will include the word "category" or "tag".

For example:

http://mydomain.com/**category**/roses/

.. might be the URL of a category page listing my posts on Roses, and

http://mydomain.com/**tag**/red

.. might be a tag page listing all posts on my site that were tagged with the word "red".

If you enter a word into the category base or tag base, when the URLs are constructed, they'll contain the category base or tag base you specified, rather than the default words, "category" or "tag".

Having keywords in your URL can be helpful, BUT, with Google on the warpath of web spammers, I would not even consider entering a category base or tag base. Leave those boxes empty.

Congratulations, you have now set up your main WordPress Settings.

Tasks to complete

1. Go through each of the items inside the settings menu and make the changes described in this chapter.

RSS feeds

We mentioned RSS feeds earlier when setting up the Reading options.

RSS feeds are an important part of your WordPress website, so I wanted to spend a little more time on this.

RSS stands for **R**eally **S**imple **S**yndication (or **R**ich **S**ite **S**ummary). An RSS feed lists information about the most recent posts on your site. This information is typically the title of the post (which links to the article on your website), and a description of it, which can be short or the entire piece.

The RSS feed is an XML document that would be difficult to read without special software, but XML is the perfect "language" to store this particular type of information.

Most web browsers can read RSS feeds and show its content as readable text. Here is an RSS feed from a website on "juicing", as displayed in my copy of Google Chrome:

Current Feed Content

Measuring heat with the Scoville Scale
Posted: Fri, 12 Oct 2012 18:20:17 +0000

Chili heat is measured on the Scoville scale

The World's Hottest Chili
Posted: Thu, 11 Oct 2012 15:01:00 +0000

What happens when you eat the world's hottest chili pepper? Watch this video and find out

Health benefits of the Jalapeno Chili pepper
Posted: Thu, 11 Oct 2012 10:32:57 +0000

I love tabasco sauce. There is something about the spicy taste that is addictive. Since I found out about the health benefits of capsaicin in chilies, I have been enjoying even more tabasco and started growing my own chilies.

Antioxidant 2011 Championships
Posted: Mon, 08 Oct 2012 21:11:00 +0000

Some interesting experiments with Asdtaxanthin. The second experiment with egg yolks is quite incredible.

You can see the summaries of the last 4 posts on my site.

Each entry has the title of the post which is hyperlinked to the article on my site. Under the title is the date and time of the post and then a short description under that.

This is much easier for humans to read than the raw XML code. Here is the raw XML for just the first item in that RSS feed:

```
<feedburner:feedburnerHostname xmlns:feedburner="
http://rssnamespace.org/feedburner/ext/1.0">http://feedburner.google.com
</feedburner:feedburnerHostname>
<item>
    <title>Anti-inflammatory juice</title>
    <link>http://juicingtherainbow.com/2380/recipes/anti-inflammatory-juice/</link>
    <comments>
    http://juicingtherainbow.com/2380/recipes/anti-inflammatory-juice/#comments
    </comments>
    <pubDate>Fri, 14 Jun 2013 09:42:46 +0000</pubDate>
    <dc:creator>Andy Williams</dc:creator>
    <category><![CDATA[Recipes]]></category>
    <guid isPermaLink="false">http://juicingtherainbow.com/?p=2380</guid>
    <description><![CDATA[Inflammation is one of the main causes of disease, and a
    lot of the foods we eat contribute to the inflammation.  With chronic
    inflammation comes disease.  This juice is a powerful anti-inflammatory drink,
    and it's tasty too.]]></description>
    <wfw:commentRss>
    http://juicingtherainbow.com/2380/recipes/anti-inflammatory-juice/feed/
    </wfw:commentRss>
    <slash:comments>0</slash:comments>
</item>
<item>
    <title>Carrot pulp salad</title>
    <link>http://juicingtherainbow.com/2320/recipes/carrot-pulp-salad/</link>
    <comments>http://juicingtherainbow.com/2320/recipes/carrot-pulp-salad/#comments
```

Every post in the RSS feed has an entry like this.

RSS feeds provide an easy way for people to follow information they are interested in.

For example, if someone was interested in juicing, they could take the RSS feed from their favorite juicing websites and then add them to an RSS reader, like the free Feedly.com for example.

Using a tool like Feedly, you can follow dozens of RSS feeds of interest. RSS used this way allows you to scan hundreds of articles by title and description, and only click through to read the ones that you are really interested in.

That is why we have RSS feeds on our site.

WordPress has multiple RSS feeds

WordPress has a main RSS feed at **mydomain.com/feed**. Type that into your web browser substituting mydomain.com for your real domain name, and you'll see yours. However, WordPress also creates a lot of other RSS feeds.

For example, an RSS feed is created for each category of posts on your site. If you have a category called "roses", then there will be an RSS feed showing just the posts in the roses category.

To find the URL of any feed, simply go to the category page on the site and add **feed** to the end of it, like this:

.. and it will display the feed for that category:

Juicing The Rainbow » Cancer [+add to my feedly]

Be the first follower (served in 322ms)

FEB 01 2012

Carcinoid Tumors
Carcinoid tumors grow slowly and affect the gastrointestinal tract and lungs. While juice therapy is not recommended for this type of cancer, there are juices you should avoid.
Juicing the Rainbow » Cancer / by Andy Williams / 512d

Cancer of the Stomach
Sufferers of stomach cancer often have problems with getting enough nutrients in their diet. We take a brief look at the fruit and vegetables that may help.
Juicing the Rainbow » Cancer / by Andy Williams / 512d

Cancer of the Ovaries
Ovarian cancer doesn't often provide strong symptoms. Juicing can help provide support from this type of cancer, but only ONE type of juice.
Juicing the Rainbow » Cancer / by Andy Williams / 512d

NOTE: The feed in the screenshot above is being displayed by a Google Chrome plugin called Feedly News Reader. If you use Google Chrome, you can find this plugin in the Chrome web store (it's totally free):

https://chrome.google.com/webstore

Other RSS feeds created by WordPress include RSS feeds for tag pages, author pages, comments, search results, and so on. You can read more about WordPress RSS feeds here if you're interested:

http://codex.wordpress.org/WordPress_Feeds

RSS feeds can help our pages get indexed

Since RSS feeds link back to our website, we can get some backlinks to our pages, which in turn help them get found by the search engines. The backlinks you get from these RSS feeds are very low quality, so they won't affect your search engine rankings much, but they do help get content indexed quickly, so it is worth submitting your main site feed to an RSS Directory like Feedage.com.

Search Google for **RSS feed submission** and you'll find more sites you can submit your main feed to. I recommend only submitting it to 3 or 4 of the top RSS feed directories though.

When you next post a new article to your site, the feeds on your site are updated, which in turn updates the feed on Feedage, which now includes a link back to your new article. The search engines monitor sites like this to find new content, so your new article is found very quickly.

Tasks to complete

1. Go and have a look at Feedly.com and signup for a free account. Subscribe to some feeds that are of interest and look through them to find articles that appeal to you. This will give you a good idea of how feeds can be helpful.

2. At the moment, because you have no content on your site, you won't have any meaningful feeds. However, as soon as you start adding content to your site, find the feed URLs where that content appears (main feed, category feed, tag feed, author feed & search feed).

User Profile

When someone comes to your website, they often want to see who is behind the information. Your user profile in WordPress allows you to tell your visitors a little bit about yourself.

In the Dashboard, hover your mouse over the **Users** link in the navigation menu and then select **Your Profile**.

Your user profile should then load. If you see a list of users instead of the profile, it means you clicked the **Users** link, so just click on your username to get to your profile.

At the top of the Profile screen you'll see a couple of settings:

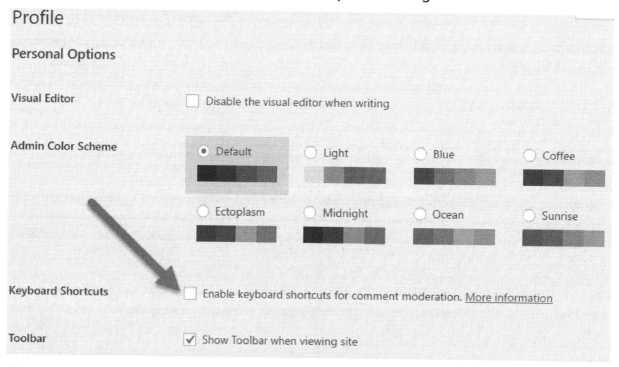

The top box should be left unchecked as we want the visual editor to be displayed when we are writing content. We'll cover that later in the book.

The Admin color scheme – choose whichever you prefer. As you check an option, your Dashboard color scheme will change to reflect your choice. You may be spending a lot of time in your Dashboard, so choose a color scheme you like.

I don't use keyboard shortcuts for comment moderation, but if you are not a mouse person, then you might like to enable this and follow the "more Information" link to learn how to use it.

What is important on this screen is the **Show Toolbar when viewing site**. We will look at that later, but for now, make sure it is checked.

The next set of Profile options are for your name:

Name

Username	Andy
First Name	Andy
Last Name	Williams
Nickname *(required)*	Andy
Display name publicly as	Andy Williams ▼

Your username cannot be changed. It will be whatever you chose when you installed WordPress.

Enter your real first and last name (or your persona name if you are working with a pen name).

Under nickname you can write anything. I typically use my first name.

The **Display name publicly as** field will be the name used on each page of your web site telling the visitors who wrote the article. Here it is on the Hello World post:

Hello world!

Welcome to WordPress. This is your first post. Edit or delete it, then start writing!

Andy

August 23, 2016

Edit

My name is actually a link to my author page, which shows all articles I have written on the site. Incidentally, that author page also has its own RSS feed (see earlier).

The next few options are contact information.

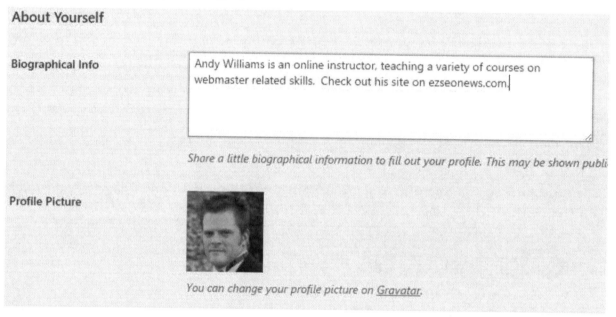

The only one that is required here is the email address and we have talked earlier about how important that is. If you want to fill out the website field, you can, but this is more useful if you have multiple authors on your site, each with their own personal website.

Next in your profile is your **Biographical Info**.

I recommend you fill in a short biography as some themes will show this on the author page. You can also see my profile picture in the screenshot. Chances are you won't have your photo there, as it needs to be setup on the Gravatar website. We'll look at that later in the book.

The author bio isn't displayed on the author page for the Twenty Sixteen theme, so here is a screenshot from my ezseonews.com website author page:

Andy Williams

About Andy Williams

Dr. Andy Williams is a Science teacher by training, but has now been working online for over a decade, specializing in search engine optimization and affiliate marketing. He publishes his free weekly Internet Marketing newsletter with tips, advice, tutorials, and more. You can subscribe to his free daily paper called the Google Daily and follow him on Facebook orTwitter. You can also follow me on Google +

EzSEO Newsletter #353 – Optimizing for Google's RankBrain

You can see my author bio at the top which is pulled from my Bio in the user profile. My posts on the site are then listed below my bio.

Also, note how my photo is included? Let's see how to do that now.

Gravatars

A Gravatar is simply a photograph or image that you can connect to your email address.

Sites that use Gravatar information, like WordPress, will show that image whenever possible, if you contribute something.

For example, your photo will show on your author page. It will also show on any WordPress site where you leave a comment (assuming you use that photo-linked email address when leaving the comment). Some themes can even show your photo after each post along with your author's bio. Here is the box that appears after every post of mine on the ezseonews.com website:

About Andy Williams

Dr. Andy Williams is a Science teacher by training, but has now been working online for over a decade, specializing in search engine optimization and affiliate marketing. He publishes his free weekly Internet Marketing newsletter with tips, advice, tutorials, and more. You can subscribe to his free daily paper called the Google Daily and follow him on Facebook orTwitter. You can also follow me on Google +

View all posts by Andy Williams →

OK, let's set this up.

Go over to Gravatar.com and find the button or link to sign up. As I write this, there is a button (but this will change, so have a look around if you don't see it).

Create Your Own Gravatar

FOR SITE OWNERS

Fill in your email address and a username and password in the form and click the **Sign Up** button.

Gravatar.com will send an email to your email address. You need to open it and click the confirmation link to activate your new Gravatar account.

On clicking that link, you'll be taken back to a confirmation page telling you that your Wordpress.com account has been activated. You can then start using Gravatar by clicking the Sign in button.

When you log in you will then be taken to a screen that allows you to assign a photo to your email address:

Manage Gravatars

1. Pick email to modify

Add email address

Whoops, looks like you don't have any images yet! Add one by clicking here!
If you don't assign a Gravatar to your email address, a custom one will be dynamically generated f
settings of the website it appears on.

Just click the link and you'll be able to choose an image from a number of different places, including upload, from a URL and from a webcam.

Once you've selected your image, you'll get an option to crop the image, so don't worry if there is other stuff in the photo that you don't want included. Just crop it out when given the chance.

You now need to rate your image (remember, we mentioned Gravatar ratings earlier when setting up WordPress):

Just click the appropriate button.

That's it. Your Gravatar should now be attached to your site's email address. Now, whenever you leave comments on a WordPress site, use that email address and your image will show up along with your comment (assuming they haven't turned Avatars off).

OK, in the next section we'll start to improve the visual aspects of our website by looking at themes, headers and much more.

Tasks to complete

1. Go and claim your Gravatar.
2. Log into your Wordpress site and complete your user profile.
3. Find a WordPress site in your niche, and go leave a relevant comment. Watch as your image appears next to your comment.

Tools

The Tools menu has three options:

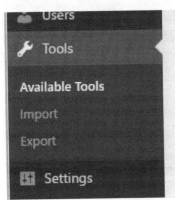

The **Available Tools** screen offers you a few tools. The first is "Press This".

"Press This" is something that most people don't use. However, I will show you how it works and what it is for.

Essentially this is an easy way to add content to your site. Imagine you are on another website, reading a fantastic article and you decide you'd like to mention this article on your own site. The "PressThis bookmarklet" gives us a quick way of doing that.

To use the Bookmarklet, click and drag the Press This button in your WordPress Dashboard up to the bookmarks bar of your web browser and drop it there. Here it is in my own browser:

Let's see what happens when I am on a site that I want to talk about on my own site.

After navigating to a site that I found very interesting, I clicked the Press This button in my bookmark bar:

Perfect French Fries Recipe : Ree Drummond : Food Network

| | Visual | Text |

B *I* ☰ ☰ **"** 🔗 ✂

Get the recipe for Perfect French Fries via @FoodNetwork:

Source: *Perfect French Fries Recipe : Ree Drummond : Food Network*

📌 Format Standard	>
📁 Categories	>
🏷 Tags	>

Publish ∨

A window opens with the title of the post already filled in (using the title of the page I want to talk about), plus a link to the post in the main post editor. I can add my own commentary to the post and the link will credit the source of the information.

When you have finished adding your own commentary about why you found the page so interesting, or why your visitors should go and read it, click the **Publish** button to add the post to your own site.

On the available tools page, you'll also find the **Categories and Tags Converter.**

Categories and Tags Converter

If you want to convert your categories to tags (or vice versa), use the Categories and Tags Converter available from the Import screen.

This helps make categories into tags and vice versa. This functionality needs to be installed separately as a WordPress plugin. Clicking on the link will take you to the Import screen which has a link to a number of different tools, including the Categories and Tags Converter. If you want to use this or any other plugin on the import screen, I suggest you read the **Details** for the plugin by clicking the link under the plugin title.

The Tools menu also has Import and Export features. These allow you to move content from one blog to another. I have used it when I wanted to merge two or more websites into one larger website. Use the export to get the posts, pages and/or media off one site, then use the import to get that data into the new site.

Let's see the process.

To Export content, click the Export menu:

Export

When you click the button below WordPress will create an XML file for you to

This format, which we call WordPress eXtended RSS or WXR, will contain you

Once you've saved the download file, you can use the Import function in and

Choose what to export

⦿ All content

This will contain all of your posts, pages, comments, custom fields, terms, navic

◯ Posts

◯ Pages

◯ Media

Download Export File

You can then choose what to export. All content, or choose between posts or pages. If you select posts (or pages), you will be given more options including categories to export, export by author, date range or status (published, scheduled, draft, etc.).

You will then click the export button to download the export file to your computer.

To Import, install the Wordpress plugin that is linked to from the Import screen:

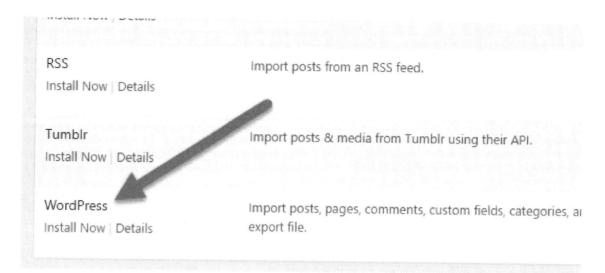

Click the Install Now link.

You can now import the file that was previously exported. You'll notice that the link under the plugin has changed to **Run Importer**.

Click the Run Importer link and you'll see the following screen:

Choose the file and click **Upload file and import.**

Appearance menu

If you click on the Appearance link in the Dashboard Navigation sidebar, it will open up to expose you more menu items:

This menu gives you access to settings that control how your website looks. It specifically relates to the template or theme you are using.

Clicking on the Appearance menu actually opens up the themes setting page.

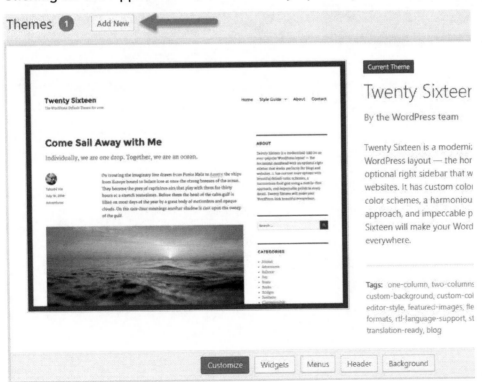

At the top of the themes screen, you have the option to **Add New** theme, which will search the Wordpress theme repository for approved (and therefore generally safe) themes that you can install and use on your site.

NOTE: You will often hear people referring to WordPress themes as templates. While the two things are not totally the same thing, people often use the words interchangeably to mean the same. So for the purpose of this book, templates and themes are the same thing.

If you have more than one theme installed, the active theme will appear first on the themes page. There will also be a search box at the top to help you search your installed themes.

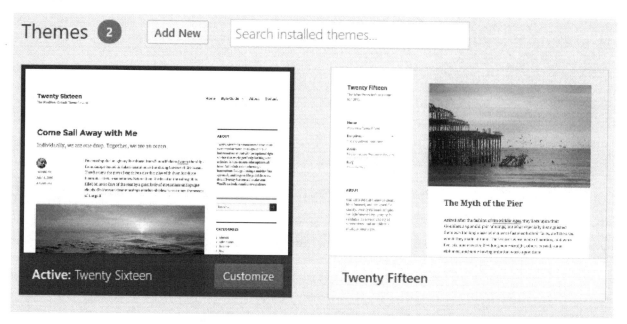

The currently selected theme is shown in the first position, with a **Customize** button next to the text **Active: Twenty Sixteen** (or whatever your active theme is called).

The customize button will take you to a WYSIWYG editor allowing you to make some design changes to the appearance of your site.

Click on the customize button to open the editor:

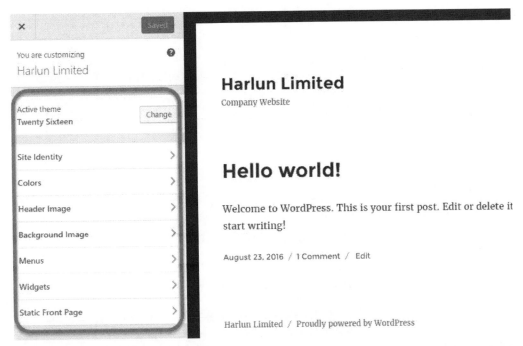

On the left is a menu that gives you access to certain configuration settings. On the right, the large window shows a preview of how your site will appear with the currently selected settings. Make changes and watch the preview update as you design how your site will look and feel.

At the top of the menu is Site Identity. If you click on that, you'll get access to these settings:

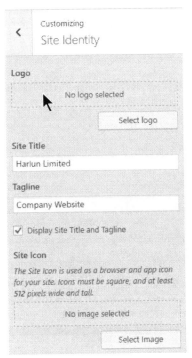

You can edit the site title and tagline and watch the preview display on the right side update with the new settings.

The one setting that is new here is the **Display Header Text** checkbox. If you uncheck this, see what happens to the preview. The Site name and tagline disappear. Try it.

Why might you want to remove the Site title and tagline?

You might decide to include the title and tagline within a header image/graphic instead so have no need for the text.

When you have finished playing around with the settings, click the arrow (<) in the top left to move back up one level in the sidebar menu system.

The next menu is the colours menu:

At the top you'll see a drop down box offering **Base Colour Schemes**.

Try the various colour schemes and watch the preview panel.

Play around with the other colour settings to see how they display in the preview screen. You can change colours by clicking the **Select Colour** button and then choosing from the palette.

If you go back up to the main menu again, **Header Image** is the next item in the list.

This allows you to upload a header image to be used across the top of every page on your site. If you do decide to use an image, make sure you turn off the Site Name and Tagline text (see earlier). Adding a header image is as easy as uploading it and cropping if necessary.

The next menu is the **Background Image** setting. This will place a background image on your page web pages (you can tile the image so it is repeated vertically and horizontally if you want). The image won't obscure the text, as the text is placed on a separate later in the foreground. Here is an example of a tiled background image of a union jack flag on my test site:

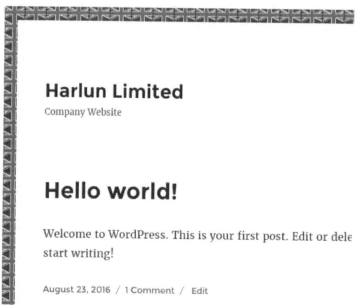

72

There are a number of options you have for these background images:

Background Repeat

○ No Repeat

◉ Tile

○ Tile Horizontally

○ Tile Vertically

Background Position

◉ Left

○ Center

○ Right

Background Attachment

◉ Scroll

○ Fixed

Background repeat allows you to repeat the image over the entire background by tiling over the whole background (along both the x and y axis), tiling horizontally (only a single layer of the image on the x axis) or tiling vertically (single layer of the image along the y axis).

The next option down is to position the background in a certain position – left, centre or right. This will determine where the image is positioned before any tiling takes place. For example, if you choose right, and have chosen to tile vertically in the repeat options, then the image will be repeated in a single column down the right side of your webpage.

The final options are to either have the background image fixed, which means it stays where it is when you scroll through the content, or scroll, which means the background image scrolls (moves), with the content.

NOTE: If you choose to have the image fixed, it may not display as fixed in the actual preview pane. Therefore, save the changes and then go to your homepage URL. Here you will be able to see the fixed image effect.

I don't recommend using a background image at all. Simply colour is better as images often look messy and unprofessional. However, I do recommend you upload an image and play around with the settings to see what they do. When you have finished, click the remove image to get rid of it.

The next item is the **Menus** settings. These allow you to select menus to use on your site. You can create menus in another area of the dashboard, and you have total control over the contents of these menus. We will look at this later.

Next up is the Widgets menu. Clicking that will open up a screen showing you the widgetized areas of your site's template. You can add/edit widgets in this screen, but I recommend you don't. The **Widget** screen in the Appearance menu is far easier to use as you will see later in this book.

If you have created a page on your site, then you will see one more option in the Customize menu - **Static Front Page**.

Customizing

Static Front Page

Your theme supports a static front page.

Front page displays

⊙ Your latest posts

◯ A static page

These options are identical to the ones we saw earlier in the **Reading Settings**.

We will look at this later.

NOTE: If you haven't created a WordPress PAGE, then you won't see this option here, or in the reading settings.

OK, when you have finished playing with the customize settings, either save and publish your changes if you like the look of your site, or cancel to undo your experimentation.

Let's now go back and see how we can install new themes to completely change the look of our website.

Finding Wordpress Themes, Installing and Selecting them

We had a brief look at installing themes earlier in the book, so we should know how to search for, and install a new theme.

Click on the **Themes** link under the **Appearance** menu if it is not already selected.

Click on the **Add New** button at the top of the themes screen.

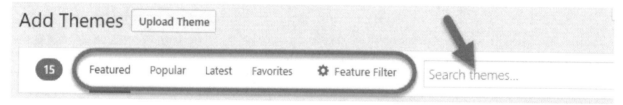

At the very top of this screen is a button, labelled "Upload Theme". If you bought, or downloaded a theme from a website, it will come as a zip file. You can install it by clicking this button, selecting the file, and clicking Install.

There is a search box on this screen which is really useful if you know the name of the theme you want to install.

There is also a menu at the top, with "Featured" selected by default. This will show you a list of the currently "featured" themes, which you can install.

Click on the "Popular" link to be offered a list of the most popular Wordpress themes. This is often a good place to start, since these are the themes that have been downloaded the most, or rated the highest.

If you want to see the latest Wordpress themes to be accepted into the theme repository, click the "Latest" link.

The next item on the menu is **Favourites** but that will be empty if you haven't favourite any themes.

Finally, the "Feature Filter" gives you the chance to specify exactly what you are looking for.

Layout	Features	Subject
☐ Grid Layout	☐ Accessibility Ready	☐ Blog
☐ One Column	☐ BuddyPress	☐ E-Commerce
☐ Two Columns	☐ Custom Background	☐ Education
☐ Three Columns	☐ Custom Colors	☐ Entertainment
☐ Four Columns	☐ Custom Header	☐ Food & Drink
☐ Left Sidebar	☐ Custom Menu	☐ Holiday
☐ Right Sidebar	☐ Editor Style	☐ News

Apply Filters

Make selections by checking the boxes and then click the **Apply Filters** button. WordPress will go away and find the themes that match the features you have selected.

You will see a list of thumbnails for all themes that match your filter criteria. You can mouse over each thumbnail to get more details of the theme and to Install it.

The preview button is well worth clicking before installing any new theme. A window opens to show you a preview of the theme, with headers, fonts, bullets etc., so you know exactly what the various aspects of your pages can look like.

If you like a particular theme, you can simply install it. If not, move onto the next one. Feel free to install a few themes. If you don't like them, you can always uninstall them easily enough.

When you install a theme, it will be added to your **Themes** page inside the **Appearance** menu. From there, you can activate it, or delete it if you decide not to use it.

If you mouse over an inactive theme, you'll see buttons to **Activate** or **Live Preview** the theme.

Live Preview allows you to see what the theme will look like on your site. The Live Preview opens in the same theme customize screen we saw earlier. If you want to activate one of the installed themes, simply click the **Activate** button.

The other option you have on this thumbnail is **Theme Details**. Clicking this will bring up more details on the theme and a **Delete** link in case you want to delete a theme. How much more detail? Well that depends on the author of the theme, and how much detail they included with the theme.

NOTE: As a matter of security, I don't recommend you keep themes that you do not use. Once you have decided which theme you want to use for your site, delete all other themes using the delete link on the "Theme Details" screen.

We are going to continue working with the Twenty Sixteen theme in this book, so I'll activate it and delete the other themes that are installed.

Adding a custom graphic header to your site

OK, click on the **Header** link in the **Appearance** menu.

There is a setting here that we need to explore. Essentially it allows you to upload your own graphic for the header of your website. I always create a header image for my sites that includes the Site Title and tagline.

The only thing you need to get right is to use the correct width & height for the header image. The dimensions differ depending on the theme. This screen will tell you what dimensions you need for your chosen theme.

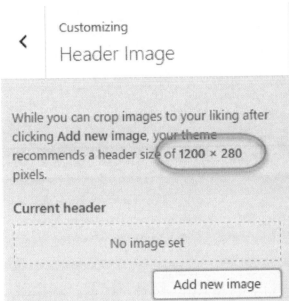

For the Twenty Sixteen theme, the image needs to be 1200 pixels wide and 280 pixels high. Any image that is not the correct size will look distorted on the site, so do stick to the suggested image dimensions.

Once you have created your image, click on the **Add New Image** button. You will be taken to a screen that has two tabs - **Media Library** and **Upload Files**.

The Media Library tab will show you all of the images that you've uploaded to your site. Chances are it is currently blank.

Switch to the Upload Files tab, and you have a choice. You can drag and drop the image from your computer into the space around the button, or click the **Select Files** button and choose the file to upload from your computer.

Once the file has been uploaded, click on the **Select and Crop** button (bottom right).

You'll then be taken to a screen showing your header with a crop box around it. Resize and reposition the crop box so that your header is central, and click **Crop Image.**

The new logo image will be inserted into your site on the preview screen so you can see how it looks. If it is OK, click the Save & Publish button top left.

Remember that if you are using a logo image, you probably want to go back to the Site Identity section of the Customize screen and uncheck the **Display Site Title and Tagline.**

Background Image

This menu will take you to the screen we saw earlier when looking at the Customize menu. It adds an image (single or tiled) behind your web page content.

The theme Editor menu

The bottom item in the Appearance menu is the Editor. This allows you to edit the theme template files. We won't be covering this in the book, as it is an advanced topic requiring programming skills.

We've skipped over two of the Appearance menu items - Widgets and Menus. These are two very important parts when designing your site, but they'll actually make a lot more sense once we have some posts published, so let's leave those until a little later on in the book.

Tasks to complete

1. Choose a theme you want to use. For your first site I recommend you stick with Twenty Sixteen (you can always change it later), as we'll use it throughout this book as our reference theme.

2. Go to the Customize screen, and try out all of the options.

3. Add a header graphic if you want to, but make sure you remove the Site Title and Tagline if you do.

Plugins

In this section, I want to explain what plugins are, where you can get them, and how to install them, etc. I'll also walk you through the installation and configuration of a few plugins as we go through this section. We will install more plugins later when there is something specific that we need on our site, but for now, let's concentrate on those that I feel are essential to all WordPress sites.

NOTE: from time to time, plugins get updated. Sometimes this is for feature enhancements, and other times it's so that the plugin remains compatible with an updated version of WordPress. Either or, there may be times where you could see different interfaces and perhaps some options removed (or added), from those illustrated in this book. Most modifications though, should be easy enough to figure out.

In the Dashboard Navigation bar, you'll see the Plugins menu. It has three options:

Installed Plugins - To view the current list of installed plugins.

Add New - For when you want to add a new plugin.

Editor - This is a text editor that allows you to modify the code of the plugins. We won't be looking at this advanced aspect.

Click on the installed plugins menu.

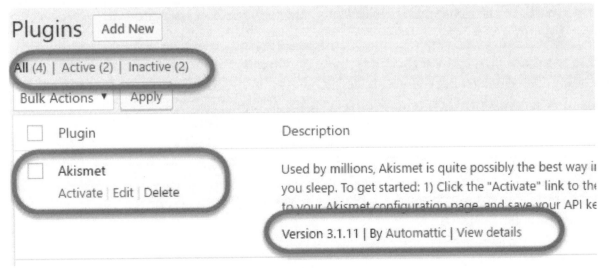

At the very top left of this screenshot you'll see where it says:

All(4) | Active (2) | Inactive (2)

If you have deactivated a plugin that was once active, you might also see a 4th group for **Recently Active**.

NOTE: You may also have a 5th group called **Drop-ins**. These are special types of plugins that alter core Wordpress functionality.

All (5) | Active (3) | Inactive (2) | Drop-ins (1)

Bulk Actions ▾   Apply

These groups refer to the plugins you have installed.

The numbers in brackets next to each of these items tells you how many plugins are in that group. We have a total of 4 plugins installed on this site, and 2 are inactive.

To activate a plugin is easy. Just click the **Activate** link underneath the name of the plugin. The menu at the top will change to reflect the new activated plugin.

Deactivating is just as easy with the **Deactivate** link.

We can view just the active plugins, or just the inactive plugins, by clicking those links.

NOTE: It is not a good idea to keep plugins installed that are inactive. If you do not need a plugin, deactivate it and a new menu item appears under the plugin title – delete. You know what to do with that!

There may be times when another group appears in this plugins menu called **Updates Available**. This will appear when there is an update available for one of your plugins and you can click this link to see which plugins have updates pending. However, I recommend you handle all updates as we saw earlier – by using the Dashboard's **Updates** menu whenever you get notified there is something that needs updating.

I don't want to use Akismet or Hello Dolly (these were pre-installed with Wordpress), so let's delete them now.

NOTE: Akismet is actually a good anti-spam plugin but it went commercial a while back, meaning it's no longer free if you have a commercial website. If you site is a free site that makes no profit, then feel free to activate Akismet.

Deleting plugins

To delete a plugin, it needs to be inactive.

To delete a plugin, just click the Delete link under the plugin name (the delete link only appears on inactive plugins):

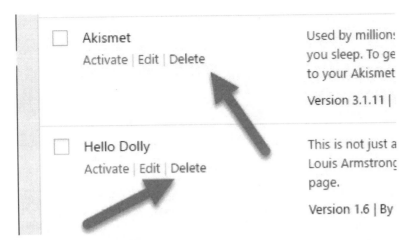

You will be asked to confirm that you want to delete the plugin:

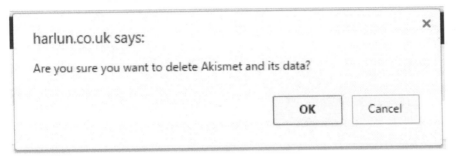

Clicking the OK button will delete the plugin and all its files from your server.

If you have more than one plugin to delete, there is a quicker way to remove multiple plugins in one go:

Just check the box next to each plugin you want to delete, then, in the **Bulk Actions** drop down box at the bottom, select **Delete**.

Now click the Apply button to carry out the deletion. You will get a confirmation screen like the one we saw a moment ago, asking you to confirm that you want to delete all of the selected plugins.

NOTE: The bulk action feature also allows you to carry out other features on multiple plugins at once. These are Activate, Deactivate and Update.

Installing important plugins

Before we look at the plugins, I need to let you know that plugins are updated frequently, and their appearance may change a little. However, these changes are usually minor cosmetic changes, so if you don't see exactly what I am showing you in these screenshots, look around. The options will be there somewhere.

Let's go ahead and install a few very important plugins, then configure them.

WP-DBManager

This plugin is VERY important because it will look after your WordPress database (that is where your website settings and content are stored). This plugin will not only keep the database healthy by optimizing it periodically, it will also make backups of the database at pre-arranged intervals, and send you a copy of the database via email. If you ever have to "reinstall" your site, these database backups are vital.

To install any plugin, click the **Add New** link in the **Plugins** menu.

On the **Add Plugins** screen, there is a search box. Type in **wp dbmanager** and hit the return key on your keyboard.

The plugin you want is this one:

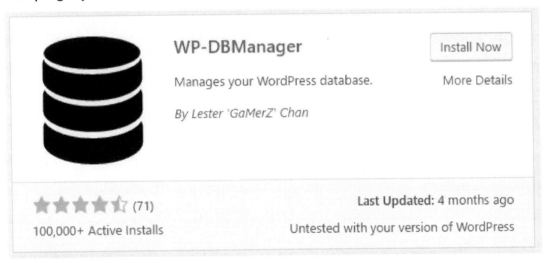

Click the **Install Now** button.

After installation, the button will have changed from **Install** Now to Activate.

Click the button to activate the plugin.

You should now see the WP-DBManager plugin in your list of installed plugins. You should see that it is active.

Whenever you activate a new plugin, you'll usually get a new menu item in the Dashboard Navigation menu. This new menu item can sometimes appear inside the existing **Settings** menu, or it can appear as a new top-level menu item. With this plugin, we get the latter:

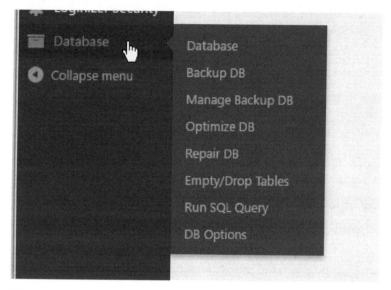

There is now a menu called "Database" in your Dashboard Navigation area.

Great. Let's configure the WP-DBManager plugin so we can start getting backups of our database emailed to us.

From the **Database** Menu, select **DB Options**.

On the **Database Options** screen, scroll right to the bottom of that page and click the **Save Changes** button (I know you didn't make any changes, but click the button anyway). By doing this, you'll activate the plugin.

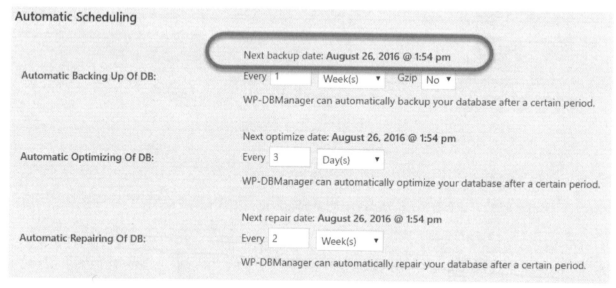

Under the automatic scheduling section, you should see today's date and (server) time. That means the first backup was created and emailed to you. It was sent to the same address found in the **Backup Email Options** "To" box on this page.

That email will be the same one we filled in earlier, but if you want to change it to a different email, you can.

If you look at the scheduling options, you'll see that a database backup will be taken once every week. If you want to change the frequency, you can. Personally, I find one backup a month is good for most of my websites, unless I am adding a lot of content, then maybe once a week is an option. I'd also recommend you change Gzip to yes, so the backup is compressed. Compressing makes the backup considerably smaller.

If you edit the settings on this screen, make sure you click the **Save Changes** button at the bottom when you are finished.

Other than that, you are all set up with this plugin.

Go check your email to see if the first backup has arrived.

Auto Terms of Service and Privacy Policy

This plugin adds a few other essential pages to the website, like the privacy policy and terms of service.

Go to the Add New plugin and search for **auto terms**.

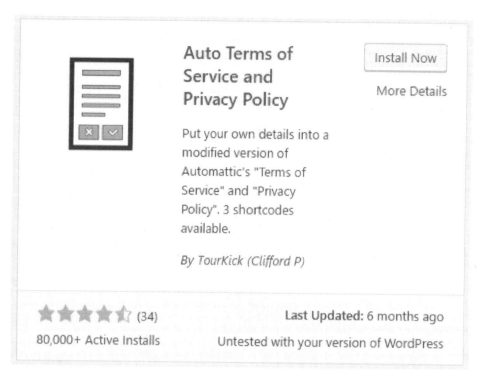

Install and activate the plugin.

This plugin installs a menu inside the main **Settings** menu.

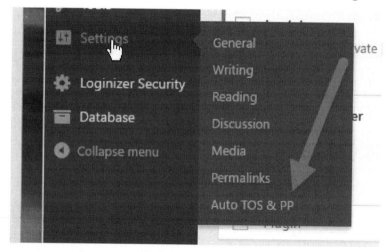

Click on the **Settings** menu followed by the **Auto TOS & PP**.

There is a form on this screen that you need to fill. It's fairly intuitive, so go ahead and fill it in.

Make sure that you have the top **On/Off** option set to **On/Displaying**, then click the Save Changes button at the bottom.

At the top of the policy options page, you have some shortcodes that you need to copy. We'll need to create two pages - one for the privacy policy and one for the terms of service document.

In the same way we created the contact page, create one page with the title **Privacy Policy** and paste in the [my_privacy_policy] shortcode.

Repeat but this time creating a terms of service page. You can give it a title or Terms, Terms of Service, or just TOS if you like. Use the [my_terms_of_service] shortcode for this one.

Once the pages are published, visit the pages to see the privacy policy and terms of service documents. Obviously these are fairly generic. If you are running a business, you might like a lawyer to look over them, or get your lawyer to create custom documents for your site.

OK; with that completed, you now have a Privacy Policy and Terms of Service page created.

Yoast SEO

Go to the **Add New** plugin page and search for **Yoast SEO**.

Install and activate the plugin.

This plugin installs a new menu in the Dashboard Navigation called **SEO**.

There are a number of options in this menu, but we'll only look at the essential ones.

The first item in the menu is **Dashboard**. If you click on that the plugin will tell you if there are any problems or improvements that can be made to your site. Across the top you will also see some tabs – **General, Your Info, Webmaster Tools** and **Security.**

The General tab gives you access to a tour of the plugin that is well worth going through. You can also **Restore Default Settings** to your site, if you end up making a mess with your SEO settings.

On the Your Info tab, you can enter a few details of your site. I recommend you do that now.

We'll ignore the Webmaster Tools and Security tabs. These are beyond the scope of this book.

The next item in the SEO menu is **Titles & Metas**. Click on it.

There are a number of tabs across the top of "Titles & Metas".

The General tab lets you change the separator symbol to be used in titles. For example, you might want to include the title of a post and the company name in your titles. It might look like this:

Are Memory Foam Mattresses Really Superior? – Sweet Dreams Limited

See the separator between the title and the company name? That is the title separator. Choose whichever one you want.

Under the title separator, you have a couple of "SEO" options enabled. With modern day SEO, I personally don't use these so disable them. If you leave them enabled, you'll see a couple of extra columns in the lists of posts and pages. Go now and look at the **All Posts** screen inside the **Posts** menu. Look at the table column headers. You'll see SEO and Readability. These two are added by those settings in the Yoast SEO screen.

The homepage, posts types, taxonomies and archives tabs define how the title and meta description are created when the web page loads. There are some other options on some of these tabs as well, which we will look at shortly.

On the Homepage tab, what you see will depend on how you have your homepage setup. If you are using a static page for your homepage, there isn't much to see on this tab, because all settings for the homepage will be defined by the page that is being used, and you'd edit the title and meta description directly in the page edit screen.

However, if you have your site setup to show the posts on the homepage, you will see boxes where you can enter title and meta description "templates".

The template is simply a set of variables which will be replaced at the time the page is rendered. Currently, the homepage title template looks like this:

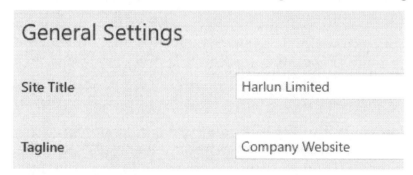

The variables all start and end with %%.

The first variable in that template is %%sitename%%. This will be replaced by the site's name when the page is rendered.

The homepage of a Wordpress site that uses blog posts for the homepage will be paginated. You might have links to 10 posts on page one, and ten page two will be created for the next 10 posts. %%page%% will insert the page number with context (e.g. page 1 of 3).

We then have the %%sep%% variable which will insert the separator character we looked at earlier.

Finally, the title template uses %%sitedesc%% which inserts the site's tagline.

If we check out my site's name and tagline in the settings:

General Settings

Site Title	Harlun Limited
Tagline	Company Website

When the homepage is loaded in a browser, the title should be "Harlun Limited – Company Website".

If we load the homepage in a browser and look at the page source, we can see it is:

```
<title>Harlun Limited - Company Website</title>
```

As you can see, the Meta Description can also be setup to use variables. You can find a full list of available variables if you click the **Help Center** link which you'll find just under the tabs. That help has two sections you should check out – **Basic Variables** and **Advanced Variables**.

I would recommend you leave the default templates settings for the homepage.

On the **Post Types** tab, you can see the now familiar template boxes for title and description of posts, pages & media on your site. Again, I would leave these default settings for title templates, but for meta description templates, I personally use %%excerpt%%. The excerpt is like a description that you can add to every post and page you create within Wordpress. We will see how to add excerpts to posts and pages later in the book. The excerpt is a natural match for the meta description of your page.

Add **%%excerpt%%** to each description template on the Post Types tab.

Posts

Title template:	%%title%% %%page%% %%sep%% %%sitename%%
Meta description template:	%%excerpt%%

Meta Robots

If a post or page on your site does not have an excerpt, then this variable will automatically generate one from the content on the page.

The other options you have for the three post types (posts, pages and media) are shown below:

The Meta Robots option will determine whether or not the content is indexed by the search engines. Obviously you want your posts in the search engines, so this should be left on **index**.

Pages are a little different to posts, especially the way I use them. We'll discuss these differences later, but just so you know, I often set the meta robots of my pages to noindex.

The second option is the Date in Snippet Preview. If you are creating a website where the date of the post is important, then you can select to show the date in the snippet preview. I personally don't create sites where the date is important, so I leave this to hide.

The final option is the Yoast SEO Meta Box. When you add a new post or page, you'll see the Yoast SEO Meta box on the edit screen:

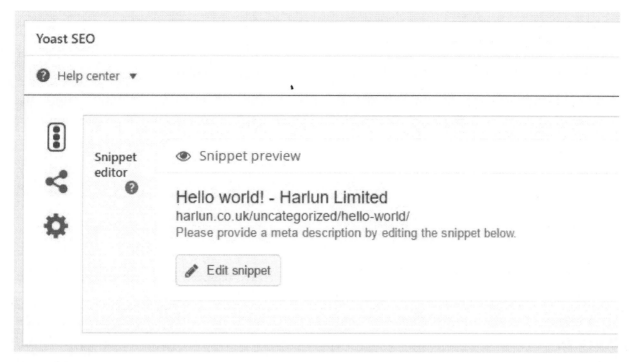

This Meta box gives us a lot of power, including the ability to override the default settings that we are currently looking at.

e.g. We have post types set to "index" in the general settings, but if we wanted to override that and create a post that we didn't want indexed, we could set the noindex from within Yoast meta box just for that one post.

We therefore want to keep the Yoast meta box option for all post types.

OK, if you have made any changes to the Post Types settings, save changes and let's look at the taxonomies tab.

The important settings on this screen are for the category and tag pages.

We haven't looked at categories or tags yet, so this may be a little confusing. For now, just leave the default title settings. There is a new variable being used in the default template, so check out the Help Center to see what the variable does.

In the Categories meta description template, as the **%%category_description%%** variable. This will insert the category description as the meta description when the page is loaded in a browser.

In the Tags meta description template, as the **%%tag_description%%** variable. This will insert the tag description as the meta description when the page is loaded in a browser.

Save your changes.

Click on the **Archives** tab. This tab contains settings for some "archive" pages, namely author and date archives plus some special pages (search & 404).

The problem with archive pages like author and date is that they can cause duplicate content in the search engines. Search engines hate duplicate content, and can penalize your site for it.

What I recommend you do is set the Meta Robots to **noindex** in both cases. You'll see the date-based is set to noindex by default, so just change the author archives setting.

Make sure you save your changes.

Before moving on, do go through the variables that have been used in these title templates. See what each variable does, so you can work out how the titles will look when a page is loaded in a web browser.

The final tab in the Title & Metas settings is the **Other** tab. This defines some sitewide settings.

The only option I am going to change is to set the **Subpages of archives** to **noindex**. This again is just to help prevent duplicate content showing up in the search engines.

OK, so that is titles & metas set up.

The next menu in the SEO settings is for **Social** integration. Click on that.

We are going to go through this quite quickly.

On the **Accounts** tab, you can enter in your social media URLs. These social profiles relate to the site, not to you personally. If you have a Facebook page for your website, then add the URL here. The same applies to all of the other social profiles – only add them if they are profiles specific to your website.

On the **Facebook** tab you have some interesting options. The open graph meta data should be left enabled. If you are not sure what meta graph is, don't worry. It basically defines what information is shared when someone shares your post on social media. It's not just Facebook that uses meta graph data, which is why we want to leave it enabled.

If you have ever shared anything on Facebook, you'll know that quite often there is an image attached to the post you are sharing. That image is taken from the web page you are sharing. With the settings on this screen, you can define a default image that will be used if there are no images within the post on your site. This is actually a good idea. You can create a small square or rectangular "logo" that will become the fallback image when someone shares a piece of your content that does not have an image.

I'm not going to go through any more of the social settings with this plugin. If you want to learn more, check out the help center, which will show you a video related to the options you are currently exploring.

On the **XML Sitemap page**, make sure the sitemap functionality is enabled (it is by default). This will create a sitemap for you, and automatically update it whenever new content is added to the site. Here is my sitemap at the moment:

XML Sitemap

Generated by YoastSEO, this is an XML Sitemap, meant for consumption by search engines.

You can find more information about XML sitemaps on sitemaps.org.

This XML Sitemap Index file contains 3 sitemaps.

Sitemap	Last Modified
http://harlun.co.uk/post-sitemap.xml	2016-08-24 12:30 +00:00
http://harlun.co.uk/page-sitemap.xml	2016-08-26 14:22 +00:00
http://harlun.co.uk/category-sitemap.xml	2016-08-24 12:30 +00:00

You can see that there are three entries. Each of these are links to a sitemap. The top one is a sitemap containing the posts on the site, the second is a sitemap to the pages on the site and the third is a sitemap to the category pages on the site.

The settings for the sitemap control what will be added to the sitemap.

For example, on the **User Sitemap** tab, the author sitemap is disabled. If you enable it, the main sitemap will then create a sitemap containing the author archives for all users of your site. Since the main goal of a sitemap is to get important pages indexed, the author sitemap is not important. All of the important pages will already be elsewhere in the sitemap.

If you click onto the **Post Types** tab, you can see that you can exclude posts, pages or media from the sitemap. Media is not in the sitemap by default, whereas posts and pages are. This makes sense for most websites, as we want posts and pages to be found by the search engines.

The **Exclude Posts** tab allows you to exclude posts or pages on a one-by-one basis. All posts and pages have an ID. It's simply a number. If you add the post ID to this box, it will be excluded from the sitemap. The easiest way to find a post ID is to go to the All Posts screen (or All Pages), and move your mouse over the post/page title. Your browser will display the post URL in the bottom left:

harlun.co.uk/wp-admin/post.php?post=1&action=edit

The post ID is the number after the ?post=

In this case, the postID is 1.

Finally, you can also exclude taxonomies (category & tag pages) from the sitemap. These are in the sitemap by default, and you can leave those default settings.

We have finished with the Sitemap settings. You can view your sitemap by clicking the **XML Sitemap** button at the top of the General sitemap settings page. The sitemap will open in a new window.

We'll be looking at other WordPress SEO settings on a post by post (and page by page) basis as we go through the book, but for now we can move on.

NOTE: Wordpress Security

I would recommend you check out a free plugin called All in One WP Security.

It is a great way to secure your Wordpress website from hackers. I'll warn you though that the plugin is quite complicated and can lock you out of the Dashboard if you set it up too aggressively. I therefore won't be covering it in this book. I simply don't want readers to face problems and then have no one to ask for help.

If you want to see a video tutorial on setting up this plugin, you can watch it here:

http://ezseonews.com/wordpresstutorials/all-in-one-wp-security-firewall/

If you want a more comprehensive look at Wordpress Security, including a more detailed set of tutorials for this plugin, I have a course called "WordPress Security – How To Stop Hackers" on.   There is a generous discount available to readers of this book on my website:

http://ezseonews.com/udemy

Note, that page lists all of my courses, so just look for the Wordpress Security course if that is the one that interests you.

Tasks to complete

1. Delete any pre-installed plugins.
2. Install WP-DBManager and set it up.
3. Install Contact Form 7 and set up a contact page.
4. Install Auto Terms of Service and Privacy Policy and create the "legal" pages.
5. Install Yoast SEO and configure it.
6. Set up the WordPress SEO plugin to handle your sitemaps.

Comments

I mentioned earlier that a lot of people turn comments OFF because they cannot be bothered with the work involved in moderating comments. The way I see it, the comments are part of the life and soul of a website and help to keep visitors engaged with you and your content. You NEED to offer them the chance to connect with you. Therefore, you really should keep comments turned on.

We have already configured the "discussion" settings to blacklist comments with known spam content (using the blacklist you found by searching on Google), but we can add another layer of protection – a comment spam plugin.

Installing a Comment Spam Plugin

NOTE: If you are running a non-commercial website, I recommend you use Akismet instead. It is probably the best anti-spam plugin available. It is for non-commercial use though, which is why we are not using it here.

Let's install that plugin now.

Mouse over the **Plugins** menu and select **Add New**.

In the search box, type **Spamshield** and hit the return key:

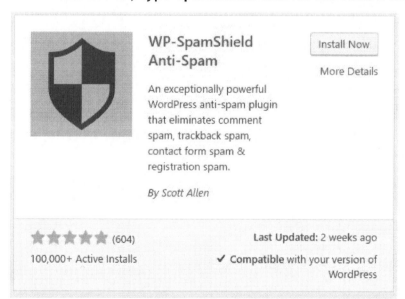

The plugin we are installing is called WP-Spamshield Anti-Spam. At the time of writing, it has over 100,000 Wordpress installs, 604 reviews and is regularly updated.

A word of warning: This plugin is not compatible with plugins that create captcha's and challenge questions. Therefore, if you use any, I would recommend you deactivate and uninstall them. They are no longer needed, as the Spamshield plugin is very powerful.

Click the **Install Now** button, and once installed, click the **Activate** button.

The plugin will create a new menu inside the Settings menu:

On the settings page there are quite a few options. We don't actually need to do anything, as the plugin is setup with default settings that should work out of the box.

Setting up the Spamshield Contact Form

It might feel like a strange place to be adding a contact form in this book, but the Spamshield plugin can create one for us. That means we don't need a dedicated contact form plugin. I always recommend you use as few plugins as possible on your site, so the Spamshield plugin kills two birds with one stone.

Scroll down the Spamshield settings page until you get to the Contact Form settings. Alternatively, you can click on the link in the table of contents to jump straight to the contact form settings.

You'll see a number of options allowing you to choose what "additional" information you want to collect from the contact form. You can choose to "include" the field on the form, or "require" the field is filled in. These are slightly different in that if a required field is not filled in, the visitor cannot submit the form.

The only option I am selecting in the list is to **Include "Website" field**. Nothing else needs changing, so scroll down and click **Save Changes**.

We now need to create a page for the contact form. Click on the **Add New** item in the **Pages** menu (not Posts).

For the title, enter **Contact**.

Now click the **Text** tab at the top right of the editor window.

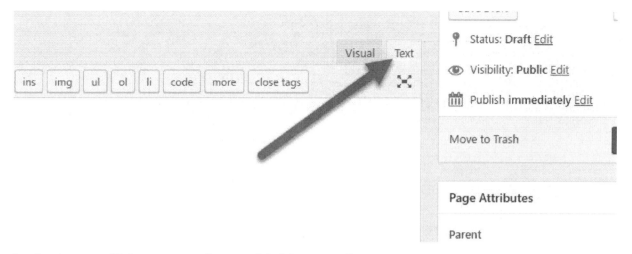

In the large edit box, enter **[spamshieldcontact]**

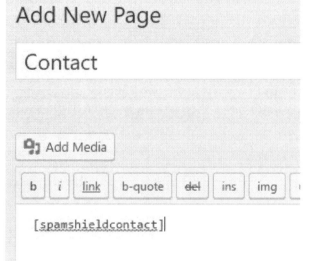

Now click the **Publish** button to save the page.

NOTE: The editor tab will stay on the Text option until you change it. It is a good idea to click on the Visual tab now, so you don't end up confused later when you want to use the WYSIWYG editor.

Once the page is published, you'll see a link to **View Page** at the top of your screen, right above the page title. Click it to view your contact form.

You now have a secure way for your site visitors to contact you.

OK; with the contact form set up, let's go back to the comments.

Moderating comments

When people comment, their comments won't go live until you approve them. This is how we set the site up earlier. If you had comments set on auto-approve, you'd most likely find so many spam comments on your site that you'd be pulling your hair out. Manual approval is the only way to go, and it does not have to take a long time.

Let's see how easy it is to moderate comments.

If you click on the Comments link in the sidebar of your Dashboard, you are taken to the comments section.

Across the top is a menu with All, Pending, Approved, Spam, Trash:

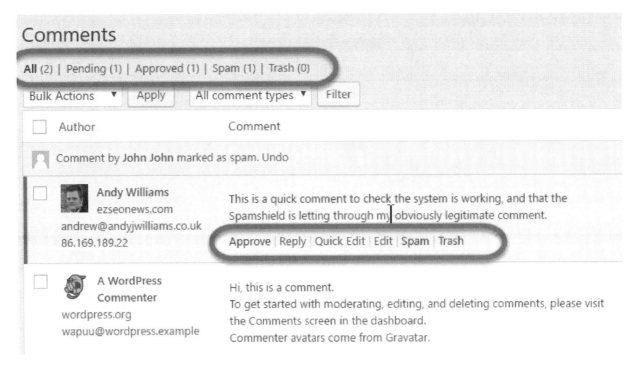

Lower down you can see a comment I added to my site. When I added the comment, I used an email address that is linked to a Gravatar, so my photo shows up. When you comment on other website's, your photo will show up too if you use a Gravatar-linked email address.

Earlier we installed the Spamshield plugin to cut back on spam comments. My comment got through OK, so passed all of the tests.

If you hover your mouse over a comment in the list, a menu appears underneath that comment, which you can click to Approve, Reply, Quick Edit, Edit, send to Spam or send to Trash.

If the comment is OK, click the Approve link. If the comment is clearly not spam, but you don't want to approve it, then click on **Trash**. If the comment is spam, click the spam link.

NOTE: Earlier in the book, I recommended you check out the **WP All-In-One Security** plugin. It has a nice feature that will automatically block comments from the IP addresses that have previously had comments marked as spam. You'll find that by using this feature, you can improve spam recognition, and make your job of moderation easier.

You can also edit comments if you want to remove something (like a link), or correct a spelling error from an otherwise good comment.

I recommend you don't reply to comments until you approve them. My typical workflow is this:

1. Moderate comments.
2. Go to the Approved comments by clicking the Approved link at the top.
3. Reply to comments that need a reply.
4. Go to the Spam & Trash folders and empty them.

In the screenshot above, you will see that there is a (1) next to the spam link. Click on the spam link to see what the spam folder contains.

You can see the comment and author for each comment in the list. If you decide that a particular comment is not spam, mouse over it and the menu appears underneath. Click the **Not Spam** link and the comment will be sent to the **Pending** pile and await moderation.

You also have the option to **Delete Permanently** if it is spam, but I rarely delete comments one at a time. You can simply click the **Empty Spam** button at the bottom to delete them all at once.

When you do delete spam, it is permanently removed.

The **Trash** folder holds all comments that were sent to the trash. Like the Spam folder, you can retrieve comments that are in the trash (if you need to), using the mouse over menu for any comment.

Finally, we have the **Approved** list. These are all comments on your site that have been approved. Click the link in the menu at the top to view them.

All comments in the Approved list have a mouse over menu as well, allowing you to **Reply** to the comment if you want to. You can of course change your mind about an "approved comment", and send it to spam or trash if you want to, or even **Unapprove** it if you want to think about it.

What kinds of Comments should you send to Spam/Trash?

You will get a number of comments that say things you like to hear, like "nice blog", or "Great job". I suggest you trash all comments like this because they are spam comments. Their only purpose is to try and get a backlink from your site to theirs.

The good news is that the Spamshield we installed later will take care of most spam. Some will get through and need moderating.

I recommend you only approve comments that:

1. Add something to the main article, either with more information, opinions or constructive information. That means never approving a comment that could have been written without that person ever reading your post. Comments MUST add something to your content. If they don't I suggest you send them to the Trash.

2. Never approve a comment where the person has used a keyword phrase for their name. You'll see people using things like "best Viagra online", or "buy XYZ online" as their name. No matter how good the comment is, trash it. What many spammers do is copy a paragraph from a good webpage on another website and use that as their comment. The comment looks great, but the name gives away the fact that the comment is spam.

3. I would suggest you never approve trackbacks or pingbacks. Most will not be real anyway.

With comments, be vigilant and don't allow poor comments onto your site as they will reflect badly on both you and your website.

Here are three spammy comments left on one of my websites. All three would go straight to the trash without hesitation:

	Author	Comment
☐	**roof cleaning ct** youtube.com/watch? v=UXHr0i7l3_A ramiro_scorfield@bigstring.c om 104.168.49.137	Very good written story. It will be helpful to anyone who usess it, as well as me. Keep doing what you are doing – i will definitely read more posts.
☐	**legendary wars Hack Tool** facebook.com/LegendaryWar sCheatsHackToolAndroidiOS jeseniahertzog@live.com 5.34.246.202	Post writing is also a fun, if you be familiar with then you can write if not it is complicated to write.
☐	**Marriage Ceremony Tips By Joe** Whoisology.com terigiorza@googlemail.com 23.232.165.73	Good info. Lucky me I discovered your blog by chance (stumbleupon). I have book-marked it for later! Approve | Reply | Quick Edit | Edit | Spam | Trash 📧 ✋ | Report to SFS

These comments are totally irrelevant to the page where they left the comment. Two try flattery to get approved! Also, check out the name of the "people" leaving each comment.

Tasks to complete

1. Install WP Spamshield Anti-Spam plugin.

2. Setup a Contact Form on your site using the built in form provided by the Spamshield plugin.

3. Whenever there are comments on your site, moderate them. Spam or Trash any comments that are not "adding to the conversation".

Media Library

Media includes things like images and video that you want to use in posts, as well as other downloads you want to offer your visitors, e.g. PDF files.

The media library is a convenient storage area for all such items.

You can go and have a look at your Media Library by clicking on the **Library** link in the **Media** menu. All items are shown as a thumbnail. Clicking on a thumbnail will open up the **Attachment Details** screen, which shows you the media item, URL, Title, etc. You even have some basic editing features if you need to crop, scale or rotate an image.

Uploading stuff to your media library is really very easy.

You will usually add media directly from the **Add Post** screen when typing a piece of content. However, if for example you have a lot of images that you want to upload at any one time, it is often quicker to do it directly in the Media library.

How to Upload New Media

Click on the **Add New** link in the **Media** menu, or on the **Media Library** page, click the **Add New** button at the top.

Uploading media is as simple as dragging and dropping it onto the large box on the screen:

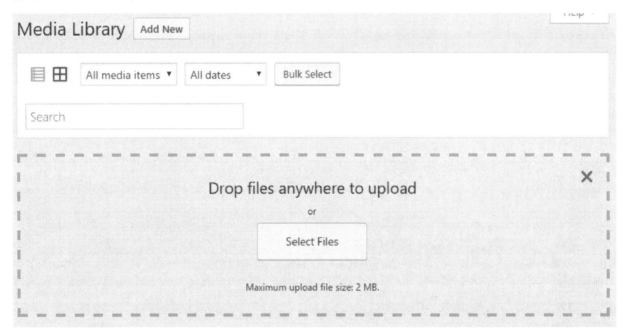

(You can also click the **Select Files** button and select them directly from your hard disk.)

To drag and drop something, simply open up the file manager on your computer. Select the file(s) you want to upload, and click and hold the left mouse button over the selected items. Now move your mouse, dragging the items to the dashed box in the Media Library screen. You can then release the mouse button, dropping those files into the Media Library.

Windows Explorer and find the item you want to upload. Click and hold on the item and drag it over to the rectangle in the media library and drop it (unclick the mouse button).

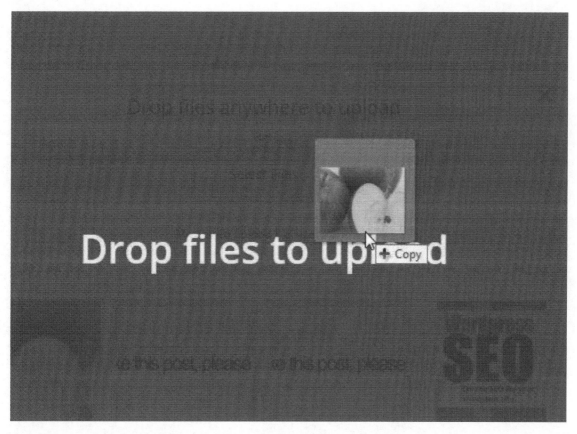

You can see I have dragged an image of apples over the box. When I drop it there, the image is uploaded to my library. When the upload is complete, you'll be shown a thumbnail of the image:

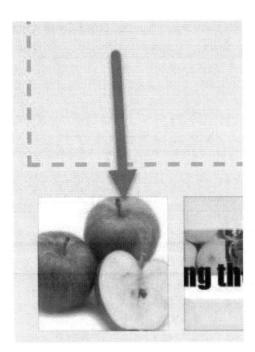

Clicking the thumbnail opens up the Attachment Details screen:

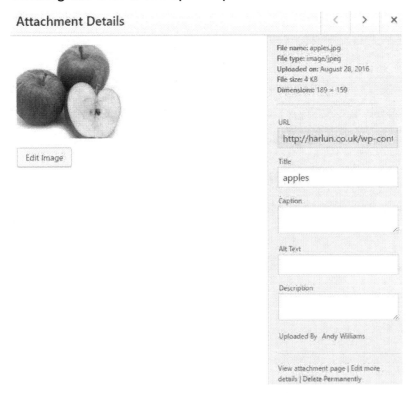

You can add/edit the image caption, title, ALT text (which is the text shown to people who have images turned off in their browsers, e.g. visually impaired or blind people who will have text to voice software in order to read the page contents), and the description.

You can also grab the **File URL** of your newly uploaded image. If you copy that and paste it into a web browser's address bar, the image will load in your browser.

We will look at how to add an image (or video), to a post later in this book. But for now, just try uploading a few images to get the hang of things. Once uploaded, grab the file URL and paste it into your browser. Do they load?

NOTE: There are some file formats that WordPress will not let you upload for security reasons. PHP files are one example. If you want to upload a file so that you can offer it as a download on your site, but it is not accepted for upload, then zip it up and upload the zipped file instead.

OK; go to your Media Library screen.

At the top, you'll see some filtering options:

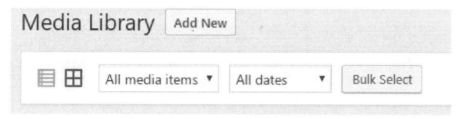

The two drop down boxes allow you to view only a specific type of media, e.g. images, or only those media items that were uploaded in a particular month.

The first two buttons allow you to view the list of media items as either thumbnails, or a table containing a little more detail. Select that first button to show the table view:

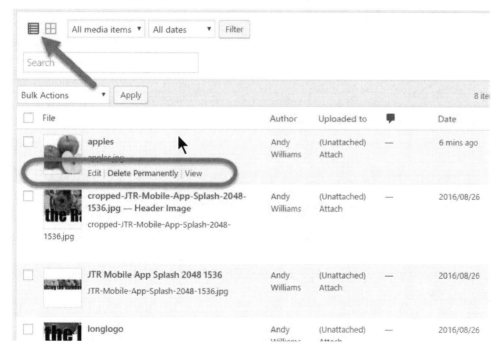

Each item has the now familiar mouse-over menu, which allows you to **Edit**, **Delete Permanently**, or **View** that media item.

There is a column showing you the date the item was added to your library.

There is also a column called **Uploaded to.** This column lets you know which page or post contains this media. If you use the image in multiple posts or pages, this column only shows the first one the image was used in.

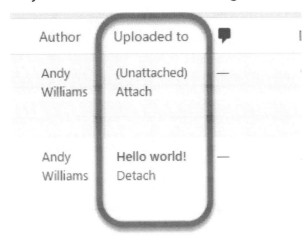

You can see that the second image in this list is attached to the Hello World post. If I click the "Hello World" link, I am taken to the post edit screen with that post loaded.

Note that columns in the media library are sortable by clicking the title of the column. Furthermore, if there are columns you don't use and don't want to see, you can hide them by using the screen options. Remember those?

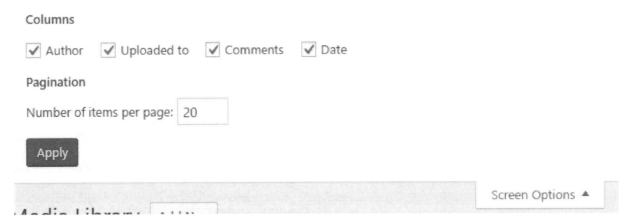

Just unclick whichever items you don't want to see. You can even specify how many media items you see per page in your library.

If you have a lot of media in your library, there is a handy search feature:

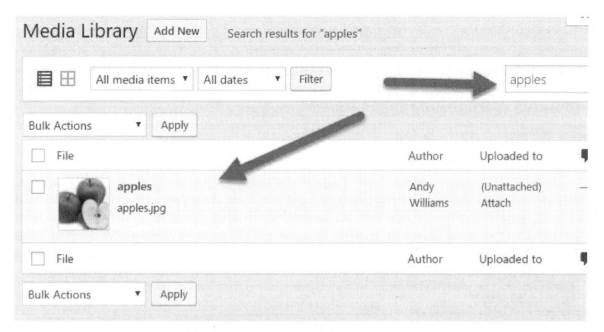

In the screenshot above, I searched for apples and the results returned the only media item called "apples". The search feature will look for your search text in both the title of the media and its description. If the word appears in either, it is shown in the search results.

The media library also gives you **Bulk Actions** (something that can be applied to multiple items in one go).

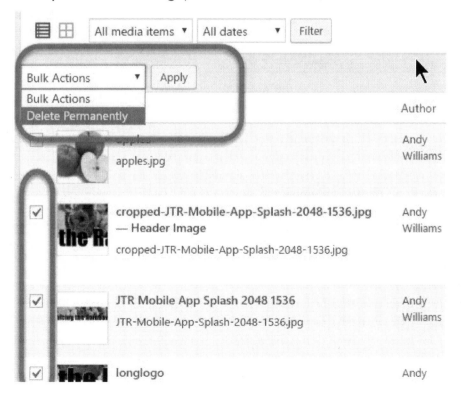

Next to each media item is a checkbox. If you want to delete several media items, you can check each one, and then select **Delete Permanently** from the **Bulk Actions** drop down box. Click **Apply** to delete the checked items.

Media Items are actually posts too!

Before we leave the media library, I should point out something interesting. Media items themselves are actually posts!

To show you what I mean, I've inserted the apples image to the Hello World post. You can see in my media library that the apples image is now attached to that post:

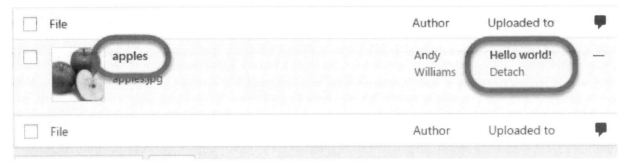

If I click on the title "Hello World", that post opens up in the editor:

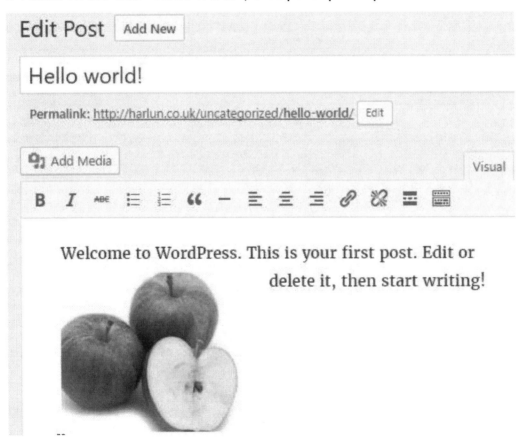

However, I can also click on the title "apples" (right next to the image in the media library table). The image then loads in the **Edit Media** screen:

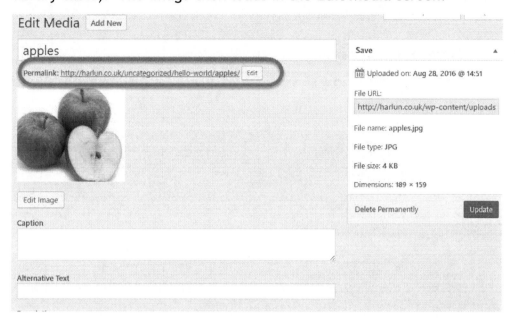

This screen allows you to edit the media caption, ALT text, description, etc. But it also displays a permalink for the image. Click on that link and you are taken to a post on your site. Go on and try it with an image in your own media library.

You'll notice that the post you are taken to has the "Leave a Reply" comments section that is found at the end of posts. This is a post on your site!

Have a look at the URL of that post. The URL will depend on whether the image is attached to a post or not. Open an image post that is attached and one that is not. Do you notice anything about the URL?

That's if for the Media Library for now. We will come back to this when we look at how to add content to your site using the **What You See Is What You Get** (WYSIWYG), document editor later.

Tasks to complete

1. Go and explore the media library. Practice uploading a photo, video or sound file and grabbing the URL.

2. Try using the search feature to find a specific piece of media in your library.

Pages v posts

When you want to add content to your site, you have two options. You can either create a new **Page** or a new **Post**. In terms of adding/editing, these two are very similar, but they are handled very differently by WordPress.

This may sound confusing to people who are new to WordPress (or maybe even new to website building). After all, isn't a post on your site a page? Doesn't a page on your site contain a post?

For some reason, WordPress creators decided to name these two types of content "posts" and "pages" and it does cause confusion. However, you DO need to understand the basic differences between them when it comes to building your site. The information I'll give you later will make it easy for you to decide which to use, so don't get hung up on these differences.

Since WordPress was originally designed as a blogging platform (i.e. to help build websites that were constantly updated with posts about whatever was going on in that blogger's life), posts were designed for these regular updates.

WordPress **posts** are *date-dependent and chronological* and this separates them from **pages** which are date-independent and not really related to any other piece of content on the site.

Posts were originally designed to be ordered by date, with a post you created yesterday logically appearing lower down the page than a post you make today. Newer posts are inserted at the top of the page, and older posts are pushed off the bottom.

It might help to think of an example.

Suppose you were keeping a blog about your weight loss program. On day one you weighed in at 210lb, so you write about that and what you have done for the day to help with your diet. Each day you write a new entry as a kind of personal journey on your weight loss progress.

When someone comes to your site, they see the daily posts in chronological order. This means visitors to your 'blog' can follow your story logically and see how your diet is working out for you.

This type of chronology is not possible to do with pages (well it is, but it takes a lot of effort plus plugins to achieve, so why bother?). Pages do not have any defined order within a site, though they can have a hierarchy with parent and child pages. We will look at this a little later on; so don't worry about it now.

OK, so the date-dependency is one important difference between WordPress posts and pages. What else?

Well, posts can be categorized, whereas pages cannot (at least not without plugins).

Suppose you were creating a site about exercise equipment. You might have a series of reviews on different treadmills, another set of reviews on exercise bikes, and so on.

Using posts allows us to categorize our content into relevant groups. If I had 10 reviews of various weight loss programs, I could create a category on my site called weight loss programs and add all 10 reviews to this category by writing them as posts.

Putting related content into the same category makes sense from a human visitor point of view, but also from the point of view of a search engine. If someone were on your site reading a review of the Hollywood Diet, it would be easy to take advantage of the features of posts in WordPress to also highlight some of the other diet reviews you have on your site. This can be done with posts (and we'll add a plugin called YARPP later to automate this), but it is a much more manual process if you tried doing the same thing with pages.

As well as categories, posts can also be tagged. Tags are an additional way to group and categorize your content. We'll discuss tags later, but for now, just realise that they can be used to further categorise your content to help your visitors and the search engines make sense of your project. It is possible to create tags for pages as well, but once again, only with plugins. As a general rule, we try not to use plugins unless they are absolutely essential as they can slow down the loading time of a website, and possibly add security vulnerabilities if they are not well maintained by their creators.

Another great feature of posts is that they can have **Excerpts**. These are short descriptions of the article that can be used by themes and plugins to create a Meta description tag, or a description of the article in a list of related articles. For example, below is a related posts section (created using the YARPP plugin that we'll install later), on my ezSEONews website. It shows excerpts being used for the post descriptions:

Related Posts:

1. EzSEO Newsletter #353 – Optimizing for Google's RankBrain
   How to optimize your content for Google's RankBrain and other tidbits of information....

2. SEO Tip #1–Don't write content about a keyword phrase
   SEO Tip #1 of 10....

3. SEO Tip #2–Don't publish "fluffy" content
   In this short video, I'll show you a major mistake that many marketers make – they publish content that is padded, even to the extent...

If a post does not have an excerpt (e.g. if you forgot to write one), the first X words of the article itself are used for the description. Bear in mind that the first sentence or

111

two of the article does not always make the best description for the article, so I recommend you add excerpts to all posts on your site.

Another important feature of posts is that they appear in your site's RSS feed. Remember, we talked about how important that was earlier in the book. Since RSS feeds are there to highlight the most recent posts, any important new content on the site should be a post so that it can be seen in your feeds.

One of the original differences between pages and posts was that pages could use different templates whereas posts could not. This meant that different pages on your site might have totally different layouts. This was not possible with posts. However, when WordPress 3.1 was introduced, a feature called **Post Formats** was added. We will look at this feature briefly when we add a post to the site, but for now, understand that post formats allow you to change the layout of your posts, on a post-by-post basis, by selecting from a list of formats.

When to use posts and when to use pages

Not all webmasters agree on this, but I am going to give you a simple rule that will tell you when to use a post and when to use a page. This is the way I have built WordPress sites for myself and my clients for several years, and the system offers great SEO benefits as well as organizing content in a logical manner to help both visitors and search engines.

Before I tell you the rule, let me first distinguish between two types of content that you may have on your site.

The first type of content is the stuff you want your visitors to see. It'll be all of the articles you've written with the visitor in mind, and is specific to the niche of your site. We will call this type of content, **Niche Content**. This will include articles, reviews, videos, infographics, etc. that **you create for your site and your targeted audience**.

The second type of content is the stuff that you need to have on the site, e.g. for legal purposes, but you don't really care whether visitors see it or not. The only reason we put it on the site is because we need to. Typical examples would be a Privacy page, Terms of Service, Contact page, and an About Us page (although a good 'About Us' page is one exception that we should make visible to our visitors). Apart from the About Us page, these others types of pages are what I call **Legal Pages**, since the only reason they are on the site is because we are required to have them there by law, or to comply with search engine rules.

Do you understand the difference?

Here is the basic rule.

Use Posts for "Niche Content", and Pages for "Legal Pages".

It's a simple enough rule, and it will make perfect sense when we start adding pages and posts to the website. Before we can do that though, we need to look at post categories and tags.

Tasks to complete

1. Go over this section until the differences between pages and posts are clear in your mind.

2. Can you make a list of any legal pages you may require on your site?

Categories & tags

Before we can start adding posts to our site, we need to think about the way the site will be structured and how the posts will be organized within the site itself.

We have already touched on categories and tags earlier in the book, and have set up the SEO settings for these taxonomies (organization of content). Let's now have a closer look at categories and tags so that you can fully understand them and add a few to your own site.

Both categories and tags are ways to categorize your posts.

All posts MUST be assigned to a category, but posts DO NOT have to have tags assigned to them. In that respect, categories are more important than tags.

Think of categories as the main way to categorize your posts, and tags as additional ways to group your posts into topics.

Let's look at an example.

Let's consider a website about vacuum cleaners. What would the main categories be on a website about vacuum cleaners?

To answer this, just ask yourself how would you want to group the articles on your vacuum cleaner site so that related articles were in the same category?

Here are some ideas for categories:

Dyson

Handheld

Dyson Ball

Eureka

Bagless

Cordless

Hoover

Upright

Canister

Miele

HEPA filter

All of these could be categories, but then you might get to the situation where one post might fit into several categories. While WordPress encourages this, I recommend you put each post into ONE category only. Thinking about one category per post actually helps you find the best categories for your site.

Of those ideas listed above, which ones would make the most sense if a vacuum could only be in one category?

How about "bagless"?

Nope. A vacuum could be bagless, upright and a Dyson.

The obvious categories from those listed above would be the categories that would only allow a post to be in one category - the brand names. My categories would therefore be:

Dyson

Eureka

Hoover

Miele

A Dyson DC25 vacuum cleaner review could only go in one category – the Dyson category.

So what about the other terms:

Handheld

Dyson Ball

Bagless

Cordless

Upright

Canister

HEPA filter

Well, these are perfect as tags because they add a little more information/detail about the post.

For example, my review of the Dyson DC25 vacuum would be in the category Dyson, but could be tagged with ball, HEPA, bagless & upright.

The beauty of using tags is that for every tag you use, WordPress will create a page just for that tag. The tag page will list ALL posts that have been assigned that tag. In the example above, WordPress would create FOUR tag pages. One for "ball", one for "HEPA", one for "Bagless" and one for "Upright".

The "HEPA" tag page will list all vacuums on the site that have been tagged with HEPA – it helps visitors find more HEPA vacuums if that is what they are interested in.

The "Bagless" tag page would list all vacuums on the site that were bagless (and therefore tagged with that term). A visitor on my site looking for a bagless vacuum could use the tag page to quickly see all available bagless vacuums that had been reviewed to date.

These tags also give search engines indications about our content, helping them understand what it's about so that it can rank better for related searches.

Tags are powerful. However, with that power comes some responsibility.

If you abuse tags, your site will become spammy. I have seen sites where posts have been tagged with 10, 20, 50, and even several hundred tags. Don't believe me? See this screenshot showing the tags for a post on one website I came across:

You don't need to be able to read the words in that screenshot to get the point. I've had to reduce the size of the screenshot to get all the tags into view. There are over 160 tags for that one article, and by the way, I happen to know that Google penalised this particular site.

Think about the problems of tag abuse by thinking how WordPress works and how it handles tags.

Every tag in that list will have its own tag page.

The biggest problem for that site is that many of the tags used on that post are not used on any other posts. That means there are 100+ tag pages with just a single post listed as using that tag.

To think about this in another way, if a post lists 160 tags, and this is the only post on the website, then the site will contain over 160 pages. It'll contain one post, 160 tag pages which are all nearly identical (as they all just list the same post), and a few other pages that Wordpress creates for us, which will actually be almost identical to the 160 tag pages.

The way the webmaster used tags in this example is clearly spam, and search engines hate spam. Please, use tags responsibly!

Let's look at one more example.

Think of a recipe website about puddings, desserts, cakes and so on.

You might have main categories like:

Ice cream

Cakes

Muffins

Mousse

Cookies

These are the obvious categories since a dessert will only be able to fit into one of the categories. To further classify the recipes on the site, we'd use tags which would add a little more detail about each post.

What type of tags would you use?

Stuck for ideas?

Tags usually choose themselves as you add more content to a website. For example, you might find that a lot of recipes use chocolate, or walnuts, or vanilla, or frosting (you get the idea). These would make perfect tags, because a visitor with a hankering for chocolate could visit the chocolate tag page and see a list of all ice cream, cakes, muffins, mousse and cookies that include chocolate.

Do you see how the tags help with additional layers of categorization? The tag pages become useful pages for visitors.

This is the mindset you are looking to develop as you utilize tags for your own website.

A few guidelines for using tags

1. Keep a list of tags you use on your site and make sure you spell them correctly when you reuse them. Remember, if you misspell a tag, another tag page will be created for the misspelt version.

2. Don't create tags that will only apply to one post. Remember, tags are there to help classify your content into groups. Most tags will be used several times on a site,

and its use will increase as you add more content. Only use a tag if it will be used on 3 or more posts.

3. Only pick a small number of relevant tags per post. I'd recommend somewhere between 3 – 6 tags per post, but if some need more, then that's fine. If some need less that's OK too. This is just a general rule of thumb.

4. NEVER use a tag that is also a category.

Setting up categories & tags in your dashboard

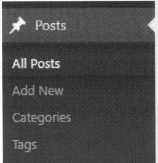

Categories and tags are properties of posts, so you'll find the menus to work with them under the **Posts** menu of the Dashboard navigation.

Categories and tags can either be set up before you start writing content, or added as you are composing it. The most common method is to set up the main categories before you begin, but add tags while you are writing your post.

I recommend that you create a description for all tags and categories, and to do that, you will need to go into **Categories** editor and **Tags** editor using the Posts menu.

OK, let's go and set up a category first. Click on the **Categories** menu:

On the right you will see a list of any existing categories.

There is only one – uncategorized. WordPress set this up for you during the Wordpress installation. Since it is currently set as the default category for posts, it cannot be deleted. We could create another category and then make it the default for posts. We could then delete the uncategorized category. However, we can just change the name of the uncategorized category so it is a useful for the site.

If you mouse over the category, you'll see a menu appear under the title (see the screenshot above).

The Quick Edit will allow you to change the category name AND the category slug. The

118

slug is just the text that is used in the URL to represent the category of the post. Remember we set up Permalinks earlier to look like this:

/%category%/%postname%/

The %category% variable is replaced by the category slug and the %postname% variable will be replaced by the post name.

Wordpress will automatically create the slug when you save your category. To create the category slug, WordPress uses the same text as the category name (converted to lowercase), with any spaces replaced by a dash.

Therefore, a category name of **juicer reviews** would have a default slug of **juicer-reviews**, but you can specify your own slug if you prefer not to use the WordPress default.

Since we want to add a description to every category we create (to be used as the category Meta description), we need to click on the **Edit** link to give us access to all settings for that category.

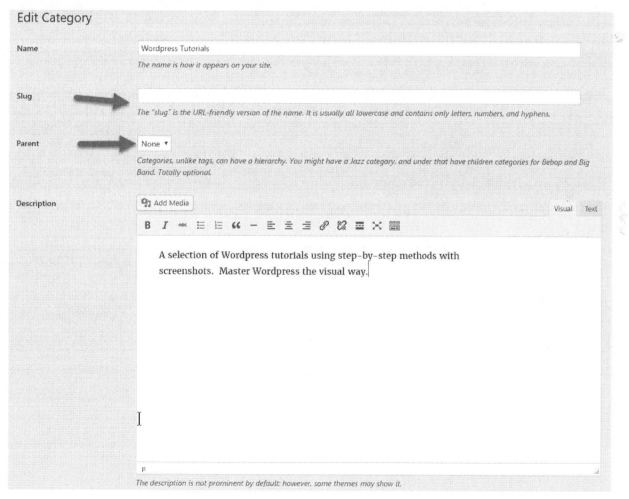

I have edited the name and slug of the uncategorized category. For the title, I replaced uncategorized with **Wordpress Tutorials.**

I have left the slug empty. When I save the category, WordPress will use **wordpress-tutorials** as the slug. That will become the text that is used in the URLs of all posts in the category.

I have added a description that will be used as the Meta description of the category page, but I have not selected a parent category.

NOTE: If you have installed the Yoast SEO plugin, you will have more options on your category edit screen. We will look at these in a moment.

With the category edited, I can click the **Update** button to save the changes. If I go back to the category screen, I can see my edited category with the new values:

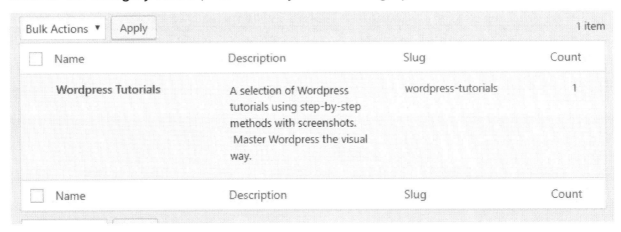

Parent categories & hierarchy

Categories can be hierarchical. In other words, you can have categories within categories.

An example might be a website on car maintenance. I might have a category called Toyota, but then want sub-categories called Yaris, Auris, Prius, Land Cruiser, etc. etc.

Therefore, the parent category would be Toyota. When I create the Yaris, Auris, Prius, Land Cruiser categories, I'd select Toyota as the parent.

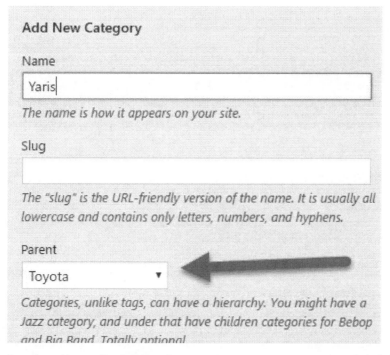

In the list of categories, you can spot parent/child relationships because parent category is listed first, with the child categories indented below:

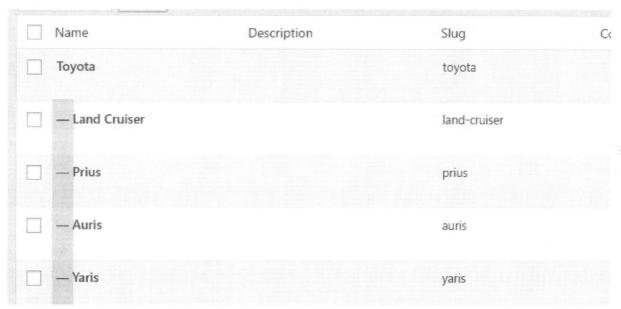

Parent/Child categories are very useful for tidying up the categorization on your site.

Imagine if you had 10 different cars from each of 5 manufacturers. That would be 50 categories for your site. That is a lot of categories to display on your site!

By using parent-child categories, you can just have the 5 main manufacturers in your menu, with the model of the cars only visible when selecting its parent.

Adding a new category

Adding a new category is easy.

Click the **Categories** menu from inside the **Posts** menu.

Fill in the title, slug (if you want to), and a description. Then select a parent if applicable. Click the **Add New Category** button and your new category is ready for use.

OK, let's look at the Yoast SEO settings for categories.

Click on **Categories** in the **Posts** menu.

Move your mouse over a category and click the **edit** link.

Scroll to the bottom of the screen, and you'll see the Yoast SEO settings.

These settings are added by the Yoast SEO plugin that we set up earlier.

This is what you'll see:

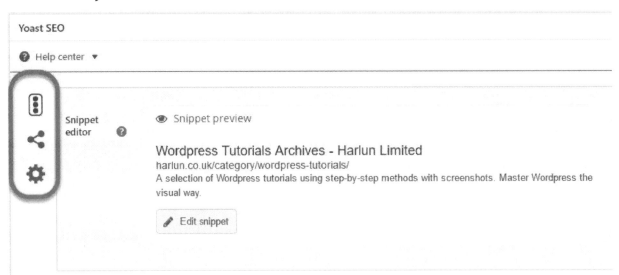

What you can see in the snippet editor is a snapshot of what your category page will look like in Google. You can see the title of the category page, URL and description (which is one reason we added a description to the category when we created it).

On the left you can see three buttons. The top one gives you access to this snippet editor. Click the **Edit Snippet** button to open up all the editing options for the category. You'll see you can change the SEO title and Meta Description using variables we looked at when setting up the Yoast SEO plugin. You are not restricted to using variables – you can type whatever you want in there. You can also edit the slug if you decide you want to.

The second button on the left is the **Share** screen, offering some settings for Facebook and Twitter. If you want to control what is written on Facebook and Twitter if someone shares the category page, then you can do so here.

The third button on the left gives you access to some useful settings.

Ignore the **Canonical URL** option -we'll let Wordpress take care of that for us.

Below this you can see the **Noindex this category** drop-down box. This allows you to tell the search engines either to index the category or not to index the category. Although this isn't something you normally want to do, it does highlight the fine level of control that this plugin adds to WordPress. We'll see more of this fine level of control when we add new content later. You should leave this as **Use category default**, unless there is a reason you want to noindex the category.

Finally, you have the option to exclude the category from the sitemap. Again, we can leave this as the default **Auto Detect**.

If you made any changes, be sure to click the **Update** button to save them.

Adding Tags

Adding Tags is very similar to adding categories except tags cannot have a parent child relationship with each other.

For every tag you enter, add a description to explain what that tag is being used for. That description will then be used for the Meta description of the tag page; this is how we set it up within the SEO plugin, remember?

Similar to the categories, the **Add Tag** screen has just a few options – Title, Slug and Description. You only need to fill in the Title and Description because WordPress will handle the slug for us. However, if you go in and edit an existing tag, you will see extra Yoast SEO plugin settings for the tag. These are identical settings to the Category edit screen, but do go in and have a look.

While I expect you will add tags directly on the **Add Post** screen as you write your content, I do highly recommend you come back to this section every time you use a new tag, just to fill in a description for those tags you create. When you make a new tag on the **Add Post** screen, you don't have the option of adding the description there and then, but it is important to add one nonetheless.

Tasks to complete

1. Set up a few categories for your site.
2. Think about possible tags and keep a list on a notepad.
3. Make sure to add descriptions to every tag and category that you add.

Writing posts

Whether you are writing posts or pages, the main content editor is the same.

To create a new post on your site, click the **Add New** link in **Posts** menu.

The **Add New Post** (and **Add New Page**) screen has a lot of information on it. Let's look at the What You See Is What You Get (WYSIWYG) Editor first.

WordPress WYSIWYG editor

The toolbar of the editor (the place where you add your content), looks like this:

If you only see one line of buttons on your toolbar, click the **Toggle Toolbar** button on the right. That will expand the toolbar.

You'll see on the top right there are two tabs – **Visual** & **Text**.

The Visual tab is where you can write your content using WYSIWYG features. On this tab you'll see text and media formatted as it will appear on the website once published. This is the tab you will want to use for most of the work you do when adding new, or editing existing content, on your site.

The other tab – Text - shows the raw code that is responsible for the layout and content of the page. Unless you specifically need to insert some code or script into your content, stick with the Visual tab.

The two rows of buttons allow you to format your content visually. If you have used any type of Word Processor before, then this should be fairly intuitive.

I won't go through the functions of all these buttons. If you need help understanding what a button does, move your mouse over it to get a popup help tooltip.

Adding content to your site is as easy as typing it into the large box under the toolbar. Just use it like you would any text editor.

Write your content. Select some text and click a formatting button to apply the format. Make it bold, or change its colour, make it a header, or any of the other features offered in the toolbar.

To create a headline, enter the headline and press the return button on your keyboard to make sure it is on its own line. Not click somewhere in the headline and select the headline from the drop down box in the toolbar.

NOTE: WordPress templates typically show the title of your post as an H1 header at the top of the page. This is the biggest header available and is equivalent to the **Heading1** in the drop down selector. You should not use more than one H1 header in your article, so DO NOT use any **Heading 1** headers as you write your content. Use **Heading 2** for sections of your article, and **Heading 3** for sub-headers inside **Heading 2** sections of your content.

OK, it's now time to go ahead and write the post, for your website.

As you write your article, you may want to insert an image or some other form of media. We looked at the Media library earlier in the book, but let's now go through the process of adding an image to an article we are currently working on.

Adding images

The process is fairly straight forward.

Position your cursor in the article where you want to add the image. Don't worry too much about getting it in the right place because you can always re-position it later if you need to.

Click the **Add Media** button which is located above the WYSIWYG editor to the left and you'll see the popup screen that we've seen previously:

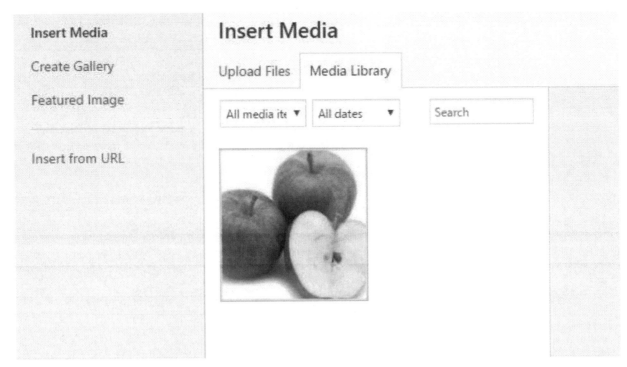

From this screen you can select an image from the media library, or click onto the **Upload Files** tab to upload a new image to the media library.

Let's add an image from our Media Library that we uploaded earlier. Click the **Media Library** tab if it is not already selected and click on the image you want to use in the post.

A check mark appears in the top right corner of the image, and the image details are displayed on the right side. These image details can be edited in the right sidebar if you want to.

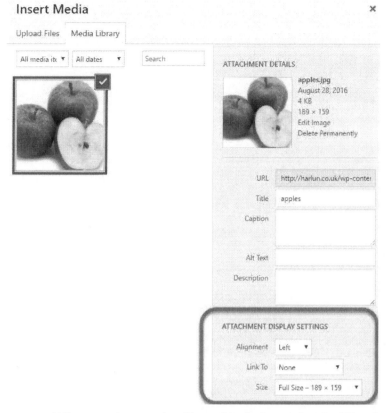

At the bottom of the right sidebar is an **Insert into post** button. Before you click that, we need to consider a few of the sidebar option.

One important option is the **Alt Text**. This text is read to visually impaired visitors to your site, and helps them understand what image are being shown. Therefore, add a short descriptive ALT text. For my example, **Red Apples** is appropriate.

At the bottom of the right hand column are some **Attachment Display Settings**. Currently my image is set to be aligned "Left". This is actually what I want. When an image is aligned left (or right) in Wordpress, the post text wraps around it. If you select **None** or **Center** for alignment, the text won't wrap.

The next option you have is to link your image to something. The default setting is **None**, meaning we insert an image that is not clickable by the visitor, because it is not linked to anything. This is the setting I use on 99% of all images I embed in posts.

You can link an image to a **Media File**, **Attachment page** or **Custom URL**.

The one that I think you will find the most useful is the **Custom** URL. This allows you to navigate to a URL when a user clicks an image. For example, if your image is a "Buy Now" button, you'd want the image linked to the purchase page.

The last of the display settings is "Size". You'll be able to choose from Full size and thumbnail. The dimensions are included with each file size, so choose the one that is closest to the size you want the image to appear in your page.

I want my image to be full sized (as I had resized the image to the correct size before I uploaded it to the media library), so I'd select **Full Size** from the size drop-down box.

Once I have made my selection, I click the **Insert into post** button at the bottom.

Here is that image inserted into my post at the position of my cursor:

If you have the position wrong, you can simply click the image to select it, and drag the image to a different location.

If you find that the image isn't inserted as you intended (e.g. you forgot to align it so the text would wrap), click on the image and a toolbar appears above the image, and a bounding box around it:

Lorem ipsum dolor sit amet, cc
sed elei
null
finil
pul\
con:
quis
con
pell
tincidunt. Nullam efficitur odic

The bounding box includes a small square in each corner. You can use this to resize the image. Simply drag one of the corners to make the image bigger or smaller.

The first 4 buttons in the toolbar allow you to re-align the image.

The last button in the toolbar will delete the image.

The toolbar edit button looks like a pencil. You can use this to open the **Image Details** screen which allows you to make a number of finer edits:

Image Details

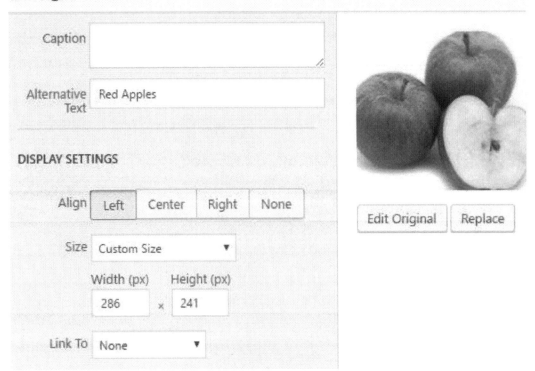

You'll also see a link to **Advanced Options** at the bottom. Click that to expand the advanced options:

The advanced option that is most useful to us is the **Open link in a new tab** option. When someone clicks the image, whatever it is linked to opens in a new browser tab.

Once you have made your edits on this screen, click the **Update** button and the changes will be updated on your post.

You can insert videos from your Media library in exactly the same way.

OK, now go on to finish your first post.

Something to try: We added an image that was already in the Media Library. Go ahead and add an image from your hard disk. After clicking the Add Media button, you'll need to go to the Upload tab to proceed. Try it and see if you can successfully add an image this way.

Once you've done that, try adding an image to a post by dragging and dropping the image from your computer directly into the WYSIWYG editor window.

It's all very intuitive.

OK; with images added, we can continue towards publishing our first article.

There are a few things we need to do before we make our article live. Let's go through the complete sequence from start, to publish:

1. Add a post title.
2. Write & format your post using the visual text editor (WYSIWYG).
3. Select a post format if available. You can ignore this option for most posts you add.
4. Select a category.
5. Add some tags if you want to. Tags can always be added later, so don't feel under any pressure to add them now. Of course, you can also decide you don't want to use tags on your site. That is fine too.
6. Add an excerpt.
7. Select a date/time if you want to schedule the post for the future.
8. Publish/Schedule the post.

OK, so we have completed down to step 2.

Post format

Not all WordPress themes use Post Formats. The Twenty Sixteen theme that we are using does and you can see them on the right of your screen:

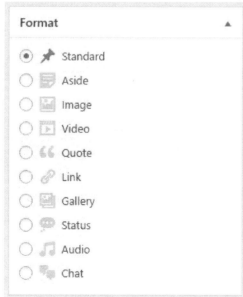

Since most, if not all of your posts, should use the default (Standard), we won't go into details in this book about other formats. Most people just won't use them and not all templates support them.

If you are interested in post formats, experiment with them. Select one and update your post. Then view your post to see how it looks. You can also read more about Post Formats on the WordPress websites:

http://codex.wordpress.org/Post_Formats

Post Category

The next step in our publishing sequence is to choose a category. Choose just one category for each post. You can add a new category "on the fly" from within the Add post screen, but if you do, remember to go in and write a description for the new category so it can be used as the meta description of that category page (remember the Yoast SEO plugin we set up earlier is expecting a description for categories and tags).

Post Tags

If you want to use tags for the post, you can type them directly into the tags box, even if they don't already exist. When you are finished typing the tags, click the **Add** button to the right of the tags box.

As you add and use more tags, you can click on the link **Choose from the most used tags** and a box will appear with some of the tags you've used before. You can just click the tags that apply, and they'll be added to the tag list of your post.

If you add "new" tags when entering a post, remember to go into the Tags settings to write a short description for each one. Yes, it takes time. However, this will be used as the Meta description of the tag page.

Post Excerpt

Next up is adding an excerpt to your post. If you look down the edit post screen, you may find that there is nowhere to enter the excerpt. That's because this option is hidden by default. Pull down the Screen Options and you'll find the box unchecked.

Check it, and the Excerpts box magically appears on your edit post screen. These settings will be remembered next time you go to add a post.

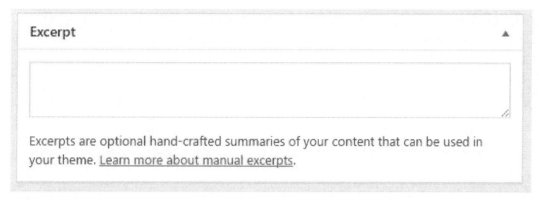

The excerpt should be a short description of the post you are writing. Its purpose is to encourage visitors to click through and read the article (e.g. From the search engine). This excerpt will be used as the Meta description tag of the post, as well as the description of the post in the "related posts" section, which is displayed at the end of each article you publish (see the YARPP plugin later).

Enter a three to five sentence excerpt to encourage the click.

Publishing the Post

OK, the next step in the process is deciding when you want the post to go live on your site.

The first option you have is to just save the post as a draft. There is a Save Draft button which you can click to do this.

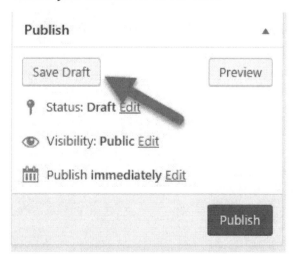

Once saved as a draft, you can go back at any time to make changes or publish the article. Draft posts are not shown on your site. To be visible on your website, you need to publish the post.

If you want it up there immediately, then click the Publish button. If, like me, you are writing several posts in a batch, it is a good idea to spread the posting of the content out a little bit. Luckily, WordPress allows us to schedule the posts into the future.

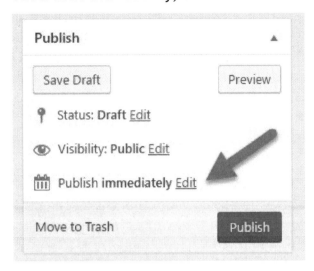

In the **Publish** box over on the right side, the default is to publish **immediately**. However, there is an Edit link that you can click which opens up a calendar for scheduling:

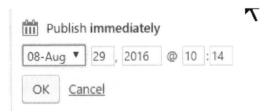

Enter the date and time you want to publish the post and then click the OK button.

The publish button now changes to Schedule.

Click the Schedule button to schedule the post.

That's it. You've just published or scheduled your first WordPress post.

Yoast SEO Settings for the Post

Before we move on, there is one last thing to cover here. It's the way that the Yoast SEO plugin is integrated into the **Add New Post** (and **Add New Page**), screen. We did look briefly at this when setting up the plugin.

If you scroll down a little, you should come across the **Yoast SEO** section.

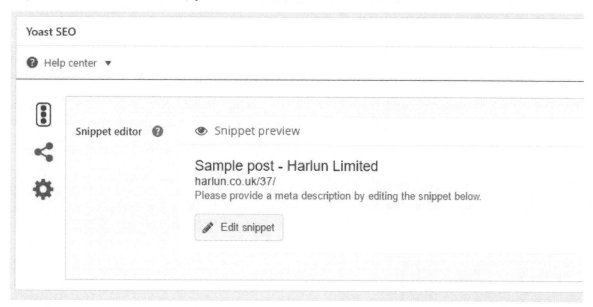

NOTE: If you don't see this section, make sure it is checked in the screen options (top right).

This Yoast SEO box looks very similar to the ones we saw for category and tag pages. The big difference is in the **Advanced** settings screen, which you access by clicking the third button down on the left (the "cog").

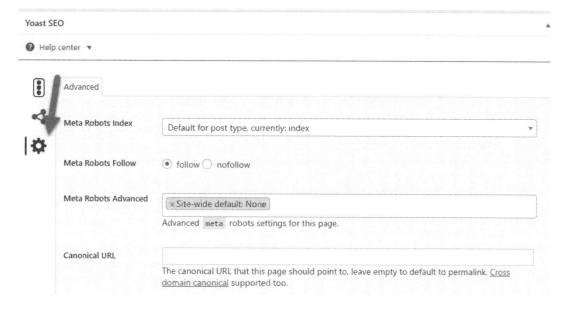

These settings give us fine control over how the search engines will deal with this post. **Not all posts, just THIS post**. With this fine level of control, we can treat every post and page on our site differently if we want to.

The top setting is **Meta Robot Index**. The default settings were set up when we installed the plugin. Essentially we want ALL posts to be indexed. If we want to make a particular post noindex, we can do it here with that top drop down box.

The next setting is the **Meta Robots Follow** option. This defines whether we want search engines to follow the links in the post. Default is yes but we can set them to nofollow. I don't recommend changing this unless you know what you are doing.

The **Meta Robots Advanced** allows us to set a few other Meta tags on our pages. Click on the edit box where it currently says **Site-wide default: None**, and a drop-down box appears with options you can set:

NO ODP can be ignored.

No Image Index is useful if you don't want the search engines to index the images on your page. Indexed images can be easily found within the image search on Google, and pirated.

No Archive tag tells Google not to store a cached copy of your page

No Snippet tells Google not to show a description under your Google listing (nor will it show a cached link in the search results).

The only options you may want to add occasionally is the **No Archive** option, but only in very special circumstances. There are times when we don't want Google to keep an archive (cached version), of a page. We can set the Meta tag to say No Archive for any post or page with these settings, thereby preventing the search engines from keeping a backup of the page.

Why might you want to do this? Well, maybe you have a limited offer on your site and you don't want people seeing it after the offer has finished. If the page was archived, it is technically possible for someone to go in and see the last cached page at Google, which will still show your previous offer.

Editing posts

At some point, after you have written a post, you may want to go in and edit or update it. This is an easy process. Just click on the **All Posts** link in the **Posts** menu. It will open a screen with a list of posts on your site.

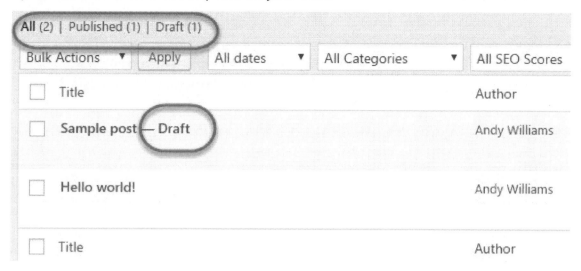

In the screenshot, you can see that I have two posts on the site. One is published, the other a draft. The draft post includes the word **Draft** next to the title in the table.

I can view just the published posts by clicking the **Published** link at the top. There is currently only one post published. I can also view just the draft posts by clicking the **Draft** link at the top. Again, there is currently only one draft post.

What if you had a lot of posts, and needed to find one?

There are two ways of doing this. One is from within your Dashboard using the available search and filtering tools. The other method is one I'll show you later by visiting your website while you are logged into the Dashboard.

For now, let's look at how we can find posts from within the Dashboard:

Firstly, if you know what month you wrote the post, you could show all posts from that month. I don't use that feature as it's easier using other methods.

You can also search for a post by showing just those posts within a certain category. Select the desired category from the Category drop down box.

Perhaps the easiest way of all is to use the Search Posts feature. Type in a keyword phrase you know is in the title, and then click the **Search Posts** button.

Once the list of matching posts is displayed, mouse over the one you want to edit and click edit rom the popup menu. An even easier way is to just click the title of the post.

This takes you back to the same editor screen you used when first creating the post. Make your changes in there and just click the **Update** button to save your modifications.

NOTE: Whenever you make changes to a post, WordPress keeps a record (archive), of those changes. At the bottom of your Add/Edit post screen is a section called **Revisions**. If you don't see it, make sure it is checked in the screen options from the top.

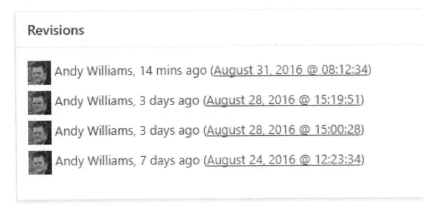

The revisions list shows all of the changes that have been made to a post, including the time stamp and the user that made the edits.

You can view any previous version of the post by clicking the date link. This does not lose the current contents; it just opens a viewer screen where you can see what that version looked like. It I click on the last revision at the top of the list (i.e. the one before the current saved version), I see this:

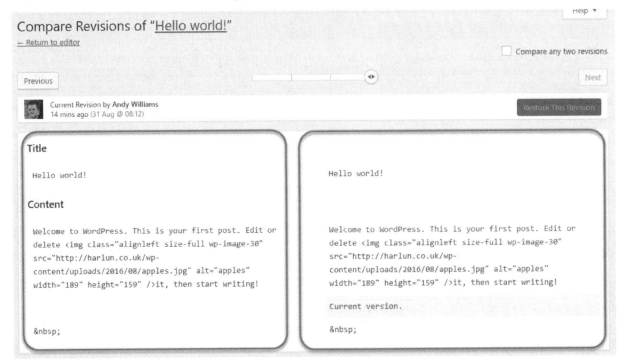

There is a link in the top left of the screen to take you back to the post editor. Click this link to cancel and return to the editor.

Below this, you can see two different versions of the post. One on the left and one on the right. These are in chronological order, with the oldest on the left, newest on the right.

Since we clicked on the last revision, we see that one on the left. The current saved post is on the right.

Differences between the two versions will be highlighted in yellow on the right (and red on the left if it is changes to specific HTML code).

At the top of the screen, you will also see a slider.

This slider will scroll through the various revisions. If I move the slider back one position, I now see this:

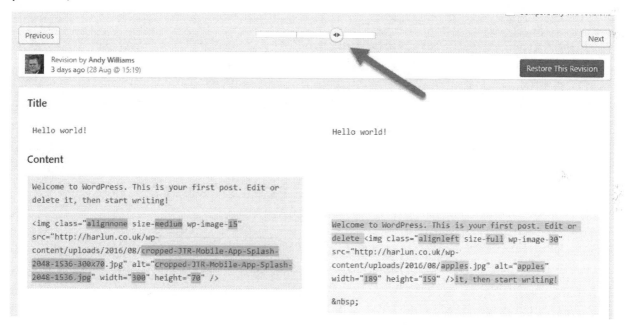

You can see the slider position at the top, and the two previews below show 3rd revision (position of the slider) on the left, and 4th revision on the right side.

Moving the slider one more position to the left will show me revision 2 and 3.

Therefore, this screen always compares two revisions that are next to each other in chronological order. However, you can compare any two revisions by clicking the check box at the top to **Compare any two revisions**.

This adds another slider and you position the first to indicate the required left side revision, and the second to indicate the required right side revision.

Go on, try it.

Why use revisions?

Suppose you are working on a post, and delete something. Later on, you ask yourself "why did I delete that?". With revisions, you can go back in an undelete.

Restoring a revision

If you find a revision you want to restore, it's as simple as clicking the **Restore This Revision** button.

This will copy the post into the editor as it was when the revision was saved, but also create a new revision of the post you are over-writing (that means you won't lose anything). When the revision is restored, you are back on the Post Edit screen, but nothing is saved until you click the **Update** button.

Tasks to complete

1. Enter a post. It doesn't have to be real post and you can always delete it afterwards. I just want you to get used to writing content in the WYSIWYG editor. Add text and an image, and then play around with the image alignment and settings.

2. Publish your post and go to your site to see how it looks in your web browser.

3. Go back and edit the post and resave (to create a revision). Repeat this a few times making changes to the post each time you do.

4. Now scroll to the bottom of the page and look at the revisions section. Check out the differences between two revisions of your post. Use the slider to scroll through the revisions. Try reinstating an earlier version and then change it back again.

Making it easy for visitors to socially share your content

Having great content on your site is one thing, but getting people to see it is something else.

One of the ways people find a website is through the search engines. They search for something and Google shows them the most relevant links. If we rank well enough for a particular search term, the web searcher may land on our page.

Another way people can find our content is via social media channels. Places like Facebook, Google plus, and Twitter are good examples. To make this more likely, we need to install a social sharing plugin on the site. A social sharing plugin will add buttons to the website that allow people to share the content they are reading by the simple click of a mouse. Social sharing buttons make sharing easy, and therefore more likely.

There are a number of great social sharing plugins, so you can actually choose whichever one you want.

Go to **Add New** in the **Plugins** menu. Search for **Social share buttons** and look for this one:

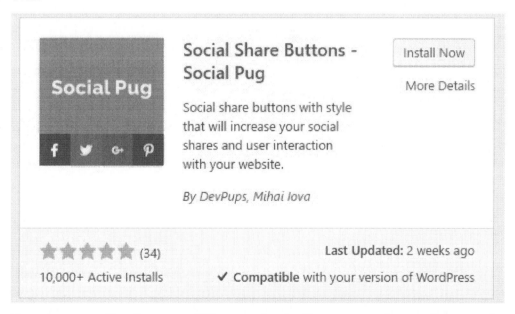

You can actually choose a different plugin if you want, but make sure that **Last Updated** was recently, and that it has a good number of high scoring reviews.

Install and activate the plugin.

You'll then find the settings for the plugin inside the **Social** Pub menu on the left.

Click that menu to be taken to the settings screen.

This particular plugin has two options. A floating sidebar and inline content:

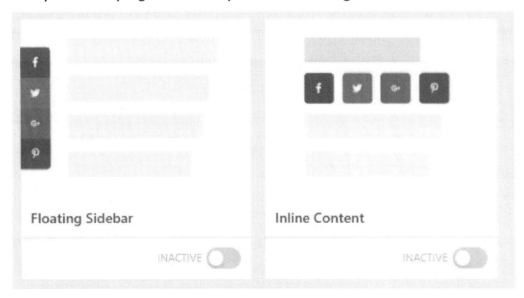

Floating Sidebar

Inline Content

Currently, both are inactive. To activate one or both, click the slider button for that option and then click on the "cog" button that appears so you can go in and edit the settings:

Floating Sidebar

ACTIVE

The first thing you'll need to do is select which social sharing networks you want to offer your visitors. On the settings screen, click the **Select Networks** button, and place a checkmark next to the networks you want:

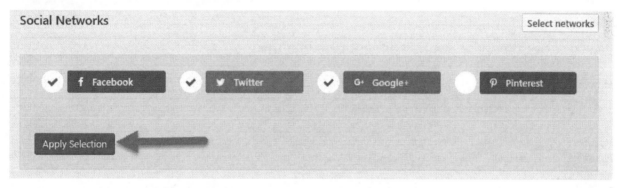

Click the **Apply Selection** button.

The networks will now appear on the settings screen, and you can re-order these by dragging them up or down using the "handle" on the left. You can also delete a network by clicking the "X" on the right.

Below you'll see some display settings. I'll leave you to explore these options. When you are ready, make sure that **Post** is checked under the **Post type display settings**, and Page is unchecked. Click **Save Changes**.

If you visit your site, you should now see the social sharing buttons. If you chose floating sidebar, it looks like this:

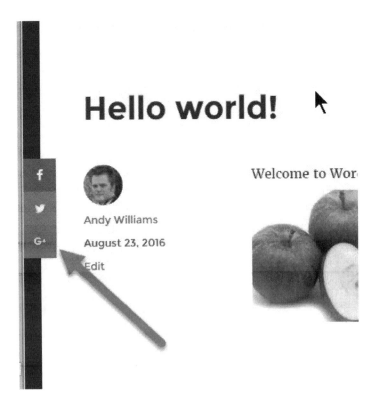

If you chose the inline content, it will look like this:

Hello world!

Andy Williams

August 23, 2016

Edit

Sharing is caring!

Welcome to WordPress. This is your first post. Edit or delete it, then start writing!

144

Obviously yours won't look exactly like mine as it depends on the settings you chose.

Other social share plugins

Over the years I have tried lots of social sharing plugins. Some work great, while others only seem to work on some websites and not others. If you find the plugin above does not work properly on *your* site, just search for "social share" in the Add Plugins screen, and try some.

Tasks to complete

1. Install the social sharing plugin and set it up to suit your needs.

Differences with pages

As we discussed earlier, pages are different to posts. On the Add/Edit Page screen, it all looks very similar, but there are a few notable omissions – namely no categories or tags! There is also no box to add an excerpt. These are no great loss to us, as we don't use pages for important articles/content on the site.

We do, however, have a couple of options for pages that are not found in posts – Page Attributes:

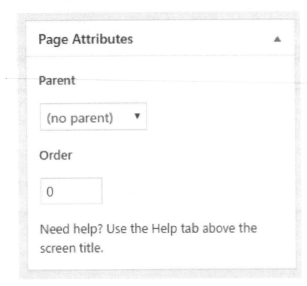

Since we are only using pages for our "legal" content (and "About" page), these new settings don't really apply to our site.

Since we won't be using this, I actually recommend that you remove the page attributes box from the page edit screen. How might we do that?

Hint: Screen Options.

Tasks to complete

1. Go and look at the Page Edit screen. Note the page attributes box.
2. Use the Screen Options to remove the Page Attributes box from the Page Edit screen.

Internal linking of posts

One of the best ways of keeping visitors on your site is to interlink the content on your pages. There are a few ways of doing this.

The basic way to add a link within your content is to highlight the word or phrase that you want to use as the link's text, and then click on the link button in the toolbar:

A popup box will appear next to the highlighted word or phrase:

If you want to link to a webpage on a different website, paste the URL into the box.

If you want to link to a post/page on the current website, type in part of the title of the webpage and Wordpress will find it for you:

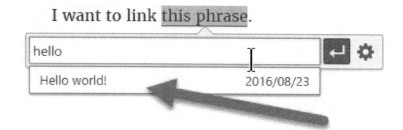

Click the post/page in the list that you want to link to. This sets the URL in the URL box. To accept the link, you can click the "Apply" button. However, before you do, you might want to change the settings of the link. To do this, click the settings button (the cog). This gives you the option to update your link details:

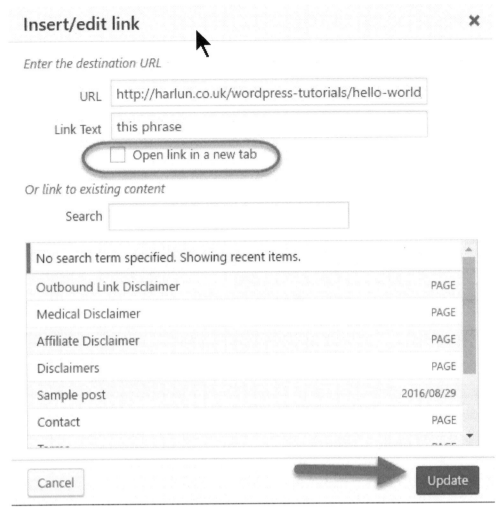

A useful option here is to check **Open link in a new tab**, especially if you are linking to another website. That way, your visitor will remain on your site, and the link target will open in a new browser window for them.

When you are happy, click the **Update** button, and then the **Apply** button to set the link.

I want to link this phrase.

If you want to edit a link, you can do this simply by clicking it.

Clicking the edit button allows you to change the link.

OK, that's the 100% manual way of inter-linking your content.

Related Posts with YARPP

One way I recommend you inter-link your content is with a plugin called **Yet Another Related Posts** plugin. This plugin allows you to set up a "Related Articles" section at the end of your posts. This will automatically link to articles that the plugin deems related (according to parameters you set up).

Go to the **Add New** Plugin screen and search for **yarpp**.

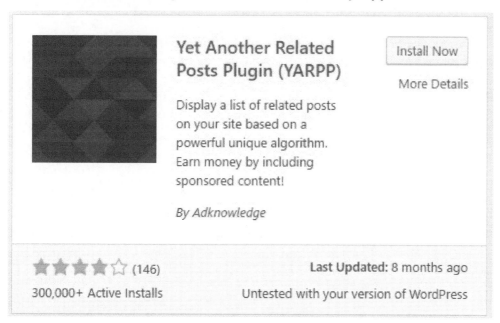

Install and activate the plugin.

You will now find the YARPP settings inside the main settings menu:

Click on the YARPP link to the settings so we can set this up.

The first thing you will notice is that at the top, there is a tab for **YARPP Basic** and another for **YARPP Pro**. We are only going to look at YARPP Basic here.

At the top of the YARPP settings, is "The Pool". The pool is the set of posts that can be used for building a related articles section. If you decide you don't want any posts in a particular category showing up in the related articles sections on your site, you can exclude that category here by checking the box next to that category.

I am going to leave the pool defaults as they are.

If you think you won't be changing these settings, you can hide "The Pool" by unchecking the option in the **Display Settings.**

The next settings on the page are the "Relatedness" options. This defines how closely related an article needs to be to be shown as a "related post" of any given post.

I recommend you leave the relatedness options with their default values. The only change I make on smaller sites is to change the Match Threshold to a 1. On larger sites, a 2 is OK.

Next up are the **Display options for your website**.

There is plenty of scope for playing around here as well, including using your own template, but we are going to again use the default settings, with one exception. Place a check mark next to **Show Excerpt?** This will give our related posts a description, which is taken from the excerpt we write. When you check that box, a few more options open up. Change Excerpt length to 25.

Before / after related entries:	`<h3>Related posts:<,` or `<div></div>`	`/` `</ol>`	*For example:* `<ol></ol>`
Before / after each related entry:	`<li>` or `<dl></dl>`	`/` `</li>`	*For example:* `<li></li>`

☑ Show excerpt?

Excerpt length (No. of words):

```
25
```

Before / after (excerpt):	`<small>` or `<dl></dl>`	`/` `</small>`	*For example:* `<li></li>`
Default display if no results:	`<p>No related posts`		

Ok, that is all we are changing. Scroll to the bottom and click the **Save Changes** button.

If you now visit your site, you will now have a related posts feature added at the end of every post on the site. You probably won't see much yet because you don't have content on the site. Here is what I see at the end of my posts on this demo site:

No related posts.

However, as you start adding content, the related posts section will start to populate with recommendations for your visitors.

Here is an example of a related posts section on one of my sites using this plugin.

Related Posts:

1. January 2016 Google Algorithm Updates
   January 2016 saw some major updates in Google, with wild swings in the rankings of many sites. What do we know about this update?...

2. Google Penguin, and other Google News
   Google's Penguin 4.0 is coming soon. What can you expect and how can you get ready for it?...

3. Finding Hot Niches
   If you have ever had problems identifying niches, or you have built a site that you thought would be profitable, and its wasn't, then Gary Harvey might have the answer with his latest offering – "Finding Hot Niches". This site is dedicated to showing you the best resources for researching...

This related posts section was on an article about search engine optimization on my ezSEONews site. Can you see the benefits? People who are reading the main SEO article are shown other articles that are related to what they've just been reading about. It gives us another chance to keep the visitor on our site.

We have looked at two ways we can inter-link our content. Firstly, we can manually create links within the content. Secondly we can use a plugin like YARPP to show related posts to our visitors.

The last option I like to use is a plugin that I can set up to control internal linking on a much more automated basis, and without losing control over the linking.

I have written an article on internal site linking using this plugin. If you are interested, you should read that article here:

http://ezseonews.com/backlinks/internal-linking-seo/

Tasks to complete

1. Go and edit an existing post, or create one for this exercise and add links manually to a couple of other pages on your site (or on another website altogether).

2. Open the page in a web browser and check that the links you added work properly.

3. Install YARPP and configure it. As you add more content to your website, check out the related posts section (found at the end of every post).

Homepage of your site - blog or static?

WordPress is a tool that was created initially for blogs. That is, websites that publish date-related content as posts. The way in which WordPress handles these posts by default is to post them on the homepage, with the latest post at the top of that page.

In the settings, we saw that we could define how many posts to include on a page with the default set at 10. That means the last 10 posts published on the site will show up on the homepage in chronological order, with the latest post at the top and older posts below. As you post more content to the site, the older posts scroll off the bottom of the homepage and are replaced by the newer ones at the top.

If that is the type of site you want, then that's fine. You can ignore this section and leave things at their default settings.

Personally, I like to create a homepage where I have more control over the content being displayed. I like to create the homepage so that it always displays my "homepage article". The homepage article is there to help visitors find their way around my site. This type of organisation is typical of non-WordPress sites. The good news is that it's easy to do in WordPress. You just need to write the "homepage article" as a PAGE, not a POST.

Once you have created that article, go to the **Reading** settings inside the **Settings** menu.

At the top of the screen there are two radio buttons with **Your latest posts** selected as default. You need to select the **A static page** option.

Now two drop down boxes will appear. The top one labelled **Front Page** is the one we are interested in. Simply click on the drop down box and select the page you created with your homepage article. I've called mine "My Homepage Article" to make it clear in this example that this will be the homepage. You should give your homepage article a useful, real title because it will appear as the title of your homepage.

153

At the bottom of your page, click on the **Save Changes** button.

OK you are all set. Go to your homepage and you'll see the main article being displayed. Here is mine:

Harlun Limited

Company Website

My Homepage Article

META
- Site Admin
- Log out
- Entries RSS
- Comments RSS
- WordPress.org

Lorem ipsum dolor sit amet, consectetur adipiscing elit. Etiam ut est at nisl consequat accumsan. Maecenas eu massa vestibulum, blandit arcu a, rutrum mi. Maecenas id mi at nunc gravida porta vitae sit amet libero. In felis erat, porttitor a ligula ut, semper eleifend nisl. Mauris pretium, elit sollicitudin condimentum aliquam, nisl nunc blandit risus, non varius nulla sem at elit. Etiam lacinia tincidunt elit a elementum. Vivamus vitae purus sit amet metus pellentesque auctor. Cum sociis natoque penatibus et magnis dis parturient montes, nascetur ridiculus mus. In gravida leo laoreet dui mollis ultrices. Morbi gravida nulla ac orci luctus blandit. Fusce mollis congue magna ac varius. Duis sit amet diam turpis. Cras mattis sem id scelerisque elementum. Mauris nunc diam, sollicitudin sed magna et,

No matter how many posts you add to your site, that homepage will not change (unless you change it).

OK, I hear your question.

"If the homepage just shows the same article, how are people going to find all my other content on the website?"

Well, that's where the sidebar, widgets and custom menus come in. We'll look at those next.

Tasks to complete

1. If you want your homepage to show the same article, create a PAGE with that article, and then go and edit the **Reading** settings to show that page on the **Front page**.

Widgets

Widgets are basically plugins that allow you to easily add visual and interactive components to your site without needing any technical knowledge.

If you want to add a list of recent posts, you can do it easily by using a widget. Perhaps you want to add a poll to your site? Well, that can be done with widgets too.

When a designer creates a WordPress theme, their initial drawing will probably have "widgetized" blocks drawn onto it, so that they can visualize which areas will accept widgets. Maybe it will look something like this example (with the shaded areas able to accept the widgets):

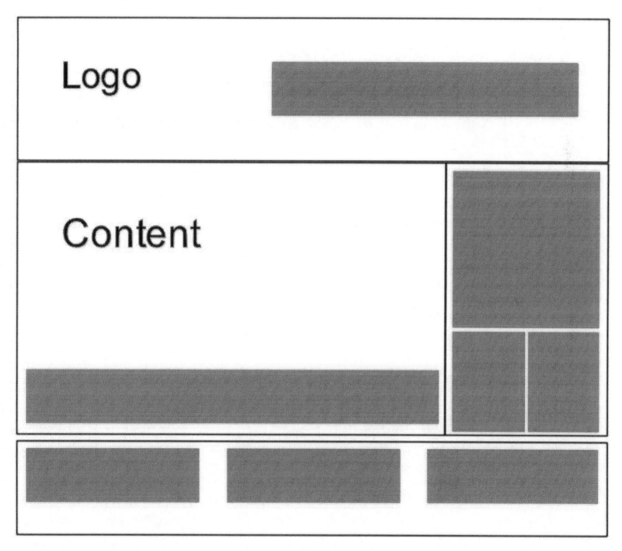

The usual areas that accept widgets are the header, sidebars and footer. Sometimes you can also add widgets after a post content.

We'll have a look at the standard widgets that come with WordPress in a moment, but first, let's see which areas of the Twenty Sixteen theme can take widgets.

Login to your Dashboard and go to the Widgets menu in the **Appearance** menu.

This will take you to an area where you can set up the widgets on your website. On the right you'll see the collapsible rectangles we looked at earlier. These represent the areas on the site that can accept widgets. As I have mentioned before, this will be different for each template, but for the Twenty Sixteen theme, this is what we've got to work with:

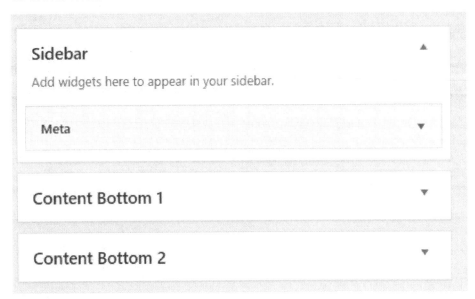

There are 3 areas of the website that can accept widgets.

Sidebar: That's the right hand sidebar that appears on all of the pages of your site.

You'll notice that there is already a widget in that area of my site. It's called **Meta**, and that adds some links to the main sidebar that you can see below:

META

- Site Admin
- Log out
- Entries RSS
- Comments RSS
- WordPress.org

If you remember, when we were clearing out the pre-installed widgets, I left that one in there so I could have a quick-link to login to my website. If I wanted to remove those links from my site, I'd simply delete that widget.

The other two widgetized areas on the Twenty Sixteen theme are Content Bottom 1 and Content Bottom 2. Thee represent areas on the left and right, situated below the content. If you want to see these areas, add a widget to the area and load a page in your browser.

To add a widget to a widgetized area, simply drag a widget from the left and drop it in the correct area on the right. On dropping the widget, it will open out with some settings you can change. Here is the category widget:

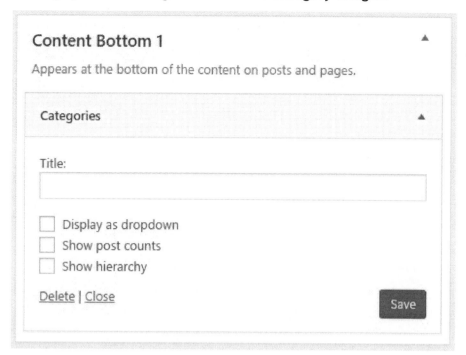

Note we can add a title. If you leave this blank, Wordpress usually inserts a default title, in this case it would be categories).

This widget also has a few settings to change the appearance of the widget. E.g. do you want categories displayed in a drop down box? Do you want categories to show how many posts per category (this is done by showing a number in brackets)? You can also show "hierarchy", so that sub-categories are indented under their parent.

Most widgets have settings, so add a few widgets, see what they do, and see what settings they have. When playing around to see what widgets do and how they appear on your site, I recommend filling in all of the settings for the widget. This will allow us to see how the WordPress template handles the formatting of the title and the text.

Here are the widgets I currently have installed in my Dashboard:

Widgets [Manage with Live Preview]

Available Widgets

To activate a widget drag it to a sidebar or click on it. To deactivate a widget and delete its settings, drag it back.

Archives	**Calendar**
A monthly archive of your site's Posts.	A calendar of your site's Posts.
Categories	**Custom Menu**
A list or dropdown of categories.	Add a custom menu to your sidebar.
End Blog Spam	**Meta**
Let others know how they can help end blog spam. </BLOGSPAM>	Login, RSS, & WordPress.org links.
Pages	**Recent Comments**
A list of your site's Pages.	Your site's most recent comments.
Recent Posts	**Related Posts (YARPP)**
Your site's most recent Posts.	Related Posts and/or Sponsored Content
RSS	**Search**
Entries from any RSS or Atom feed.	A search form for your site.
Tag Cloud	**Text**

Most of those were pre-installed with Wordpress, but can you spot the two in that list that were added by plugins we installed earlier in the book?

Answer: End blog Spam and YARPP.

Hopefully you can now see the potential of widgets.

As you've just seen, you are not limited to the widgets that come pre-installed with WordPress. Many plugins or services provide their own WordPress widgets so that you can add new features to your website as you build it. For example, the YARPP widget will add a list of related posts to ay widgetized area (usually the sidebar) in case you don't want them displayed after the post.

Basic HTML

One thing that will come in handy is some simple HTML code that you might like to use in widgets. You can add HTML to a text widget. For example, if you want to add some text with a link to another page, you'd just look up the HTML below for creating a hyperlink and insert it into your text widget accordingly.

A hyperlink

<a href="URL">LINK TEXT</a>

Just replace URL with the web address of the page you want to link to, and the LINK TEXT with the word or phrase you want linked.

Example:

If you are interested, you can read my review of the <a href="http://blenderreview.com/waring">waring blender</a> for more details.

It I entered that into a sidebar text widget, it would look like this on my site:

EXAMPLE LINK

If you are interested, you can read my review of the waring blender for more details.

I added a title to the text widget (Example link). You can see the phrase "waring blender" is a link to the URL I specified in the HTML.

An image

To insert an image, here is the HTML:

<img src="URL" width="XX" height="YY" />

Replace URL with the URL of the image (upload it via the media library and grab the URL there), XX is the width in pixels and YY is the height in pixels. If your image is the correct size (which it should be to keep image load times to a minimum), then you can leave out the height and width parameters and the code just becomes:

<img src="URL" />

For example, using an image from my media library, I grabbed the URL for the image and inserted it into a text widget. This is what it looks like:

IMAGE INSERTED

That's a 32-year-old me!

A numbered list

The HTML for a numbered list is a little more complicated.

<ol>

  <li>**item one**</li>

  <li>**item two**</li>

  <li>**item three**</li>

</ol>

You simply replace item one, item two, item three and so on with whatever you want displayed. You can add as many items as you need. Just repeat the <li>**item**</li> code once for each item you want to add.

For example, here is some code which shows a numbered list for my top three tablet recommendations.

<ol>

  <li>Asus 301</li>

  <li>Asus 201</li>

  <li>Apple iPad</li>

</ol>

.. and this is what it looks like in a sidebar text widget.

AN EXAMPLE LIST

1. Asus 301
2. Asus 201
3. Apple iPad

NOTE: The text you add for an item CAN be a hyperlink. Just construct it from the HTML I showed you above.

A bullet list

A bulleted list is almost the same code as the numbered list with one modification.

Instead of the code opening with <ol> and closing with </ol>, a bullet list opens with <ul> and closes with </ul>. The "ol" stands for ordered list (ordered by number), whereas the "ul" stands for unordered list.

<ul>

  <li>**item one**</li>

  <li>**item two**</li>

  <li>**item three**</li>

</ul>

Here is my widget now:

A BULLET LIST

- item one
- item two
- item three

That should give you enough HTML to get you started with text widgets.

There is one other widget that I do want to discuss in a little more detail. It goes hand-in-hand with one of the features we haven't looked at yet, which are custom menus. The widget itself is used to display a custom menu in a widgetized area. We therefore need a custom menu first, so that's where we'll begin.

Tasks to complete

1. Go and explore the widgets area. Add some widgets to your site and then view the site in your browser to see what they do and how they format the information.

2. Add in a text widget and experiment with the HTML code I gave you in this chapter. Try adding a text widget to the top of the sidebar with a photograph of yourself (or your persona image), and a brief bio.

Custom menus

To add or edit a custom menu in WordPress, go to the **Menus** item inside the **Appearance** menu.

Let's design a custom menu for our website. In it, we'll add links to the legal pages we created – Contact, Privacy Policy and Terms.

Add a name for your menu in the **Menu Name** box, and click the **Create Menu** button:

I've called my menu "Legal Menu" to reflect its purpose. This makes things easier when you have multiple menus and you are trying to decide which one is which from just the title.

On the left of the screen, you'll have a section that lists all Pages, Posts, Categories etc. Pull down the **Screen Options** and check Tags as well.

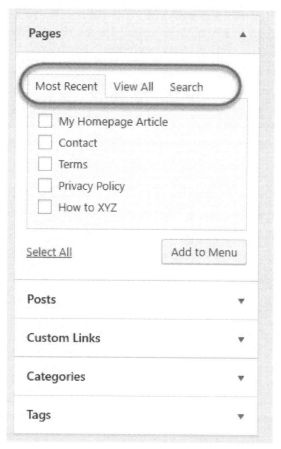

You can now add any post, page, category page or tag page to the menu.

At the moment, the Pages section is expanded. You can see three tabs at the top: **Most Recent**, **View All** and **Search**. These will help you find a specific page so you can insert it into the menu.

To expand a different section, simply click on the section. E.g. Posts:

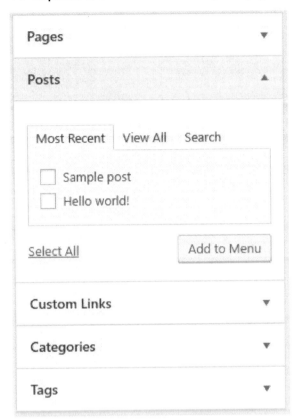

Pages collapses, and Posts opens.

Since we want to add legal pages, click on the Pages section to expand it. We want the privacy policy, terms and contact. If you can see them all in the **Most Recent** screen, check the box next to each one. (If you don't see them all in the most recent, click on view all, and you will find them there).

With all three checked, click the **Add to Menu** button:

You will see all three added to the menu on the right hand side of the screen:

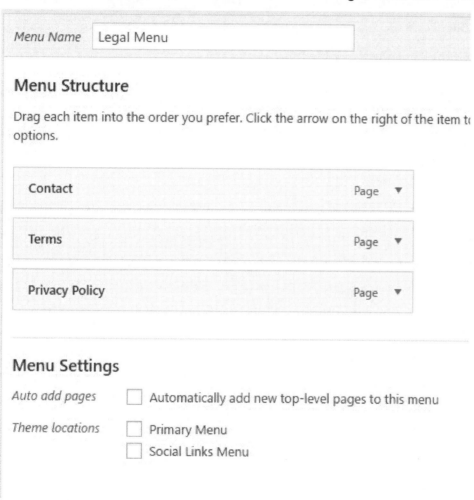

If you move your mouse over one of the items in the menu, the cursor changes:

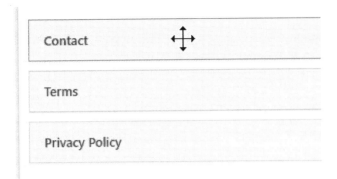

This cursor indicates that the item can be dragged and dropped. Click and drag it up or down to re-order the items in the menu. I want Terms at the top, then privacy and contact at the bottom.

Under these three menu items are two other options:

Menu Settings

Auto add pages	☐ Automatically add new top-level pages to this menu
Theme locations	☐ Primary Menu
	☐ Social Links Menu

The **Auto Add Pages** option will automatically add new pages you create on the site to this menu. That typically isn't something we want, so leave it unchecked.

The second option defines the location of the menu within the theme. The Twenty Sixteen theme has two locations assigned to menus. One is the primary menu, and the other is the social links menu.

The social links menu is a special menu that should be used for your social media links (Facebook, twitter, etc.), so we'll ignore that one. The Primary menu is across the top of the site, under the header. Check **Primary Menu** and then **Save Menu**. Now go and check out your website.

Harlun Limited
Company Website

Terms   Privacy Policy   Contact

My Homepage Article

Lorem ipsum dolor sit amet, consectetur adipiscing elit. Etiam ut est at nisl consequat accumsan. Maecenas eu massa vestibulum, blandit arcu a, rutrum mi. Maecenas id mi at nunc gravida porta vitae sit amet libero. In felis erat, porttitor a ligula ut, semper eleifend nisl. Mauris pretium, elit sollicitudin condimentum aliquam, nisl nunc blandit risus, non varius nulla sem at elit. Etiam lacinia tincidunt elit a elementum. Vivamus vitae purus sit amet metus pellentesque auctor. Cum sociis natoque penatibus et magnis dis parturient

META

- Site Admin
- Log out
- Entries RSS
- Comments RSS
- WordPress.org

CATEGORIES

You can see the menu has been added on the top right. The Twenty Sixteen theme is responsive, so if you resize your browser window and make it smaller, the menu will collapse to a "Menu" button, and clicking the button will open the menu:

Harlun Limited
Company Website

Terms

Privacy Policy

Contact

Have a play around with that. Add a menu, then resize your web browser window until the menu disappears into the menu button. Increase the size of your browser again to see the menu items re-appear.

Menu Hierarchy

It is possible to create drop-down menu within the Twenty Sixteen theme, but using a hierarchy for the links in the menu.

To do this, drag the second menu item a little to the right, so it is indented under the first one. Then repeat for the third menu item so that it looks like this:

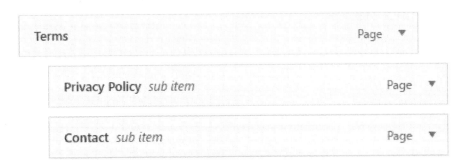

Save the menu and then visit your site again.

The menu will now just show the "parent" item, in this case **Terms**:

Terms ⌄

Moving your mouse over Terms will open the menu:

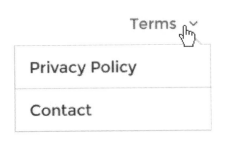

This technique can be used to tidy up big menus with lots of items.

On the Menus screen, you'll probably have noticed two tabs at the top – **Edit Menus** and **Manage Locations**. The Edit Menus screen is the one we have been working in to create this menu. The Manage Locations screen is there to make it easier to manage multiple menus and place them in the predefined locations within the template. Since Twenty Sixteen has two menu locations, you can see them both listed here, and you can choose which menu to insert into each, by selecting from the drop down box:

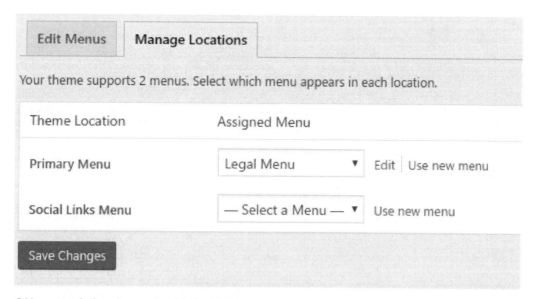

OK, switch back to the **Edit Menus** screen.

One other type of link that can be added to a menu is a custom link. You can see it listed there on the left. This allows you to link to ANY URL you like, and add that link to the menu:

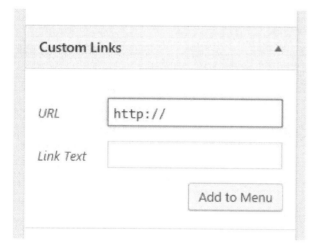

Simply add the URL of the page you want to link to, and the link text you want to appear in the menu, and click **Add to Menu**. The link will then be added to the menu.

You may have noticed that each link in the menu has a little arrow on the far right. Click it to expand the options for that link:

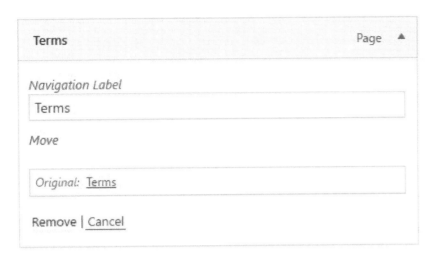

The default only provides the options shown above, but some are hidden. Open the **Screen Options** and check the options for **Link Target** and **Link Relationship (XFN)**.

You will now see two new items in the options:

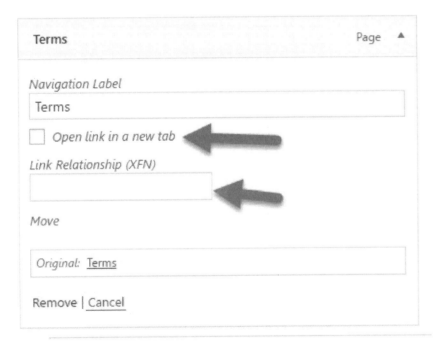

The Link target option creates the checkbox so you can choose to have menu links open in a new tab.

The Link Relationship option allows you to add nofollow tags to your links. If you don't know what these are, don't worry. Simply put, the nofollow tag tells a search engine that a page you are linking to is not important. I often use these on links to my legal pages like this:

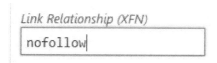

Link Relationship (XFN)

`nofollow`

Edit an existing Menu

There will be times when you want to edit an existing menu. This is straight forward enough. Go to the **Menus** screen inside the **Appearance** menu.

Use the dropdown box to choose the menu you want to edit:

Click the **Select** button to switch to that menu, and edit.

Custom Menu Widgets

OK, so one final thing. Any custom menu you create can be added to a sidebar (or any widgetized area) using the custom menu widget. I'm going to create another menu quickly so I can show you how this works.

First, I need to **Create a new menu**:

We create it the same way. Add a name for the menu (I am calling mine **Sidebar Menu**) and click the **Create Menu** button.

I'll just add a couple of posts to the menu using the Posts selector and then save my new menu.

OK, now it's time to head back to the **Widgets** screen found inside the **Appearance** menu.

When you get there, drag a custom menu widget into the Main Sidebar:

Add a title and select the menu from the dropdown box.

the widget, then check out the sidebar on your homepage. Here is mine:

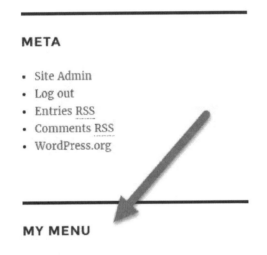

You can create custom menus for all kinds of things. These may be top review pages or important tag pages. The point is this; custom menus give you the flexibility you need as you design and develop your website.

Tasks to complete

1. Go and experiment with Custom Menus.
2. Create a menu with a "Home" link (custom link to homepage URL) and links to the "legal" pages on your site. Don't worry if you're unsure about what you want to add to the menu(s), as you can always update things later.

Viewing your site while logged in

Something special happens when you are visiting your website while logged into your Dashboard.

Earlier, when we were looking at the User Profile, we made sure an option was checked – **Show Toolbar when viewing site**. Let's have a look what happens with that option enabled.

Login to your dashboard and then open your website in another tab of your web browser.

What you'll see is a very useful "ribbon" across the top of your website:

This ribbon gives you access to some important WordPress features. For example, if you want to edit a page or post on your website, you can visit your website, find the post, then click on the edit post link in the ribbon bar (you can see it in the screenshot above). That link will open up the post in the WordPress Dashboard ready for editing.

The ribbon is very useful as you browse your site. If you find errors, just click the **Edit Post** link, fix the issue(s), and then click the **Update** button.

Three items in the menu have drop down options.

Mouse over your site name on the left, and you'll have links to:

These links will take you directly to those areas of the Dashboard.

There is also a quick way to add new content to your site. Mouse over the **New** item to quickly add a new post, page, media item or user:

If you installed the Yoast SEO plugin, that adds a dropdown menu to the toolbar too, offering quick SEO links. I'll leave you to explore those.

Finally, on the right, if you mouse over your name, you'll get this menu:

These options are self-explanatory.

The ribbon has a couple of useful indicators too. If you have any updates that need installing, the update indicator will tell you:

If you mouse over this, it will tell you what needs updating. In my case, it's a plugin. Clicking the update indicator will take you to the Update section of the Dashboard.

There is also a speech bubble that represents comments awaiting moderation. If there are comments waiting, the speech bubble will tell you how many. In my case, I don't have any comments awaiting moderation:

Clicking the speech bubble will open up the Dashboard at the moderate comments screen.

Tasks to complete

1. Login to your site.
2. Open the site in a new tab in your browser.
3. Mouse over, then click, every option in the ribbon bar at the top. See what these links do, and where they take you when you click them.

174

WordPress security

WordPress has often been criticized as being too easy to hack. There have been a lot of cases where people have lost their WordPress site after a hacker gained access to it and wreaked havoc. Several years ago, one of my sites got hacked so badly that I just deleted the whole thing and let the domain expire. At that time, I didn't have a reliable backup system in place. It is therefore wise to take the security of your site very seriously.

Earlier in the book we set up a plugin which is sending us database backups every week or so via email. That's a great start, but the plugin does not backup everything we need to restore a site. It doesn't backup the theme, plugins, or any customizations we may have made.

To create a complete backup of my sites, I use a script that I bought called WP Twin. This script creates a perfect backup of a website (which includes things like theme settings and plugins). If a site of mine ever did get hacked again, I could restore the entire project with a few simple clicks of the mouse (or even move the site to an entirely different domain).

WP Twin is a premium script that isn't cheap. Knowing that most people have a tight budget when starting out, I had a look around for a free alternative. I found one that has good reviews, but have not used it myself. It's called Duplicator and you install it the same way you do for any plugin. Just search for Duplicator in the add plugins screen of your dashboard.

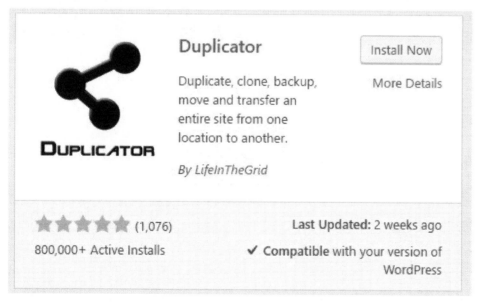

Disclaimer: I have not used this plugin so cannot show you how it works or personally vouch for it in any way.

What this plugin will allow you to do is take an exact snapshot of your site and all its data, which would then allow a complete reconstruction of the site if anything bad happened. I would keep the database backups coming via email as well, but Duplicator will provide you with another layer of cover should you ever need it.

Another layer of protection is to **always upgrade WordPress** as soon as there is a new update available.

The WordPress team fix security leaks as soon as they are found. Therefore, if your Dashboard says there is a WordPress upgrade; install it as soon as possible to make sure your copy of the software is up-to-date with any bug fixes and or new security patches.

As I mentioned earlier, I have a full video course on the topic of Wordpress Security, and how to make sure your site is virtually hack-proof. If you want more details on that, please visit:

http://ezseonews.com/udemy

That page lists all of my courses, so just look for the Wordpress Security course if that is the one that interests you.

Also, don't forget you can watch this free video I created:

http://ezseonews.com/wordpresstutorials/all-in-one-wp-security-firewall/

Tasks to complete

1. Always keep WordPress up to date.
2. Install a backup plugin, like Duplicator, and make a full backup of your site.
3. Watch the free All in One Security Firewall video from the link above, and consider setting it up to secure your website.

Monitoring website traffic

Every Webmaster wants to know how many visitors their site is getting and how those people are finding their pages (through search engines, via social media channels, etc.).

Fortunately, there are a number of good (and free) solutions to give you this information.

The tool I use on my own sites is called Google Analytics, but it is complex and perhaps overkill for someone just starting out. I'd therefore recommend you use a free service like Get Clicky:

http://clicky.com/

Setting this up is beyond the scope of this book, but it is fairly straightforward. You'll need to install tracking on your Wordpress website, so may want to look for a plugin by Yoast called **Clicky by Yoast**:

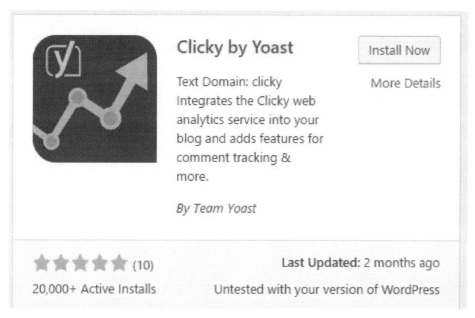

This plugin will help with the integration into your website. Once installed, Clicky will monitor the visitors on your site. You'll get information about where they come from and what they do on your site.

As your site grows, I'd highly recommend you look into Google Analytics and make the switch. It's the best free tool out there and gives a wealth of information about your visitors.

Tasks to complete

1. Install web analytics on your site. An easy option for beginners is to use the free services over at **Get Clicky**.

2. Install the Clicky by Yoast plugin and configure it as per the installation instructions on the plugin site.

3. Go over to the Clicky website and explore the tracking options. Use their Help if needed, so that you can find your way around the data and make sense of what it all means.

4. When you have time, look into Google Analytics.

Search Engine Optimization (SEO)

Search Engine Optimization has changed a lot in the last couple of years. It has always been one of the most important aspects of building a website because it helps you to rank better in Google, and consequently get more traffic and make more sales from your pages (the latter only being important if your site is commercial of course).

Today, things are very different. If you overdo your optimization, Google are likely to penalise you and dump your site out of their search engine.

If you ask Google about the best way to optimize your site, they'd probably tell you to avoid Search Engine Optimization altogether and just focus your efforts on the 'visitor experience', and not to worry about the search engines.

Despite sounding like a lost cause, you should still consider a number of "best practices" as you build your website. I will list the main things to consider here, but if you want a more in-depth discussion about SEO, I'd highly recommend my own book on the subject called **SEO 2016 & Beyond - Search Engine Optimization will never be the same again.**

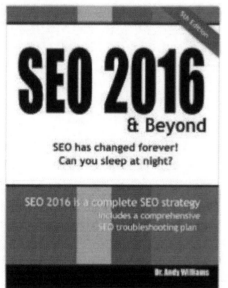

It's available in Kindle Format and as a paperback on Amazon:

Search Amazon for: **SEO 2016 & Beyond**

Alternatively, if you prefer learning by watching videos, check out my SEO course on Udemy. Just follow the link I gave you earlier in the book to the page on my site that lists my courses.

Main points for safe SEO

1. Always write content for the visitor, not the search engines.

2. Always create the highest quality content possible and make it unique. More than that, add something to your content that is not found on any other websites covering the same or similar topic, for example, your personal voice, experience or thoughts.

3. Engage your visitor, and allow them to open discussion with you via the built in comments feature.

4. Never try to write content based on keyword phrases. Always write content around a topic. E.g. don't write an article on "best iphone case", write an article on "Which iPhone Case offers the best protection for your phone?" See the difference?

5. As a measure of whether your content is good enough, ask yourself if you could imagine your article appearing in a glossy magazine? If you answer no, then it's not

good enough to publish on your own website.

6. DO NOT hire people to build backlinks to your site. If you want to build some links, create them on quality websites that point back to yours. More on this in my SEO book mentioned previously.

7. Add a social sharing plugin to your site so that people can quickly share your content on social channels like Facebook, Twitter, YouTube and Google Plus etc.

8. The best advice I can give you for present day SEO is to **read and digest Google's Webmaster Guidelines**. They are there to help us create sites that will rank well in their Search Engine Results Pages, aka SERPs. You can read those guidelines here:

http://ezseonews.com/wmg

Tasks to complete

1. Read Google's Webmaster Guidelines over and over again until you know them off by heart. They really are very important and will benefit you in the long run; providing you adhere to their suggestions of course

Where to go from here?

We've covered a lot of ground in this book. You should now be confident finding your way around the WordPress Dashboard.

You have installed WordPress, installed the essential plugins, and configured everything so that your site is now ready for content.

So what's the next step?

Create impressive content!

Everything we have done in this book has been to achieve one main goal. Get your site set up & ready to accept your content. You can now concentrate on publishing content while WordPress takes care of the rest.

Here is your plan going forward.

1. Create a post.
2. Publish it.
3. Rinse and repeat steps 1 and 2.

If you want a "static" homepage rather than one showing your recent posts, create a PAGE with the content you want displayed there. Then set up the reading settings so that this page is shown permanently on your site's front page. You can then go back to the 3-step process outlined above

Create a post, publish & repeat.

Good luck!

Andy Williams

http://ezSEONews.com

Useful resources

There are a few places that I would recommend you visit for more information.

My Other books

All of my books are available as Kindle books and paperbacks. You can view them all here:

http://amazon.com/author/drandrewwilliams

You'll find books on various aspects of being a webmaster such as creating high quality content, SEO, CSS etc.

My Video Courses

I have a growing number of video courses hosted on Udemy. You can view a complete list of these at my site:

http://ezseonews.com/udemy

There are courses on the same kinds of topics that my books cover, so SEO, Content Creation, Wordpress, Website Analytics, etc.

http://ezSEONews.com – This is my site where I offer free help and advice to webmasters. While you are there, sign up for my free weekly newsletter. You can also look through past issues and read articles on a variety of topics related to building WordPress sites.

Google Webmaster Guidelines: http://ezseonews.com/wmg – this is the webmaster's bible of what is acceptable and what is not in the eyes of the world's biggest search engine.

Google Analytics (http://www.google.com/analytics/) – the best free analytics program out there. When you have some free time to learn how to use Google Analytics, I recommend you upgrade from Get Clicky.

Please leave a review/thought on Amazon

If you enjoyed this book, or even if you didn't, I'd love to hear your comments about it. You can leave your thoughts on the Amazon website.